YOUR PURPOSE IN LIFE IS TO WIN!

How to Create and Maintain Real Life Success

SHEILA KAY

FIRST EDITION

Aristocrat Publishing (www.aristocratpublishing.com)
ISBN- 978-0-692-60019-1

For publication permissions contact:

publisher@aristocratpublishing.com

FOR LAILA

.

CONTENTS

1 PERSPECTIVE

"If you are having trouble seeing your worth, check the viewpoint from which you are looking." ~Sheila Kay

Your Purpose in Life is to Win! is a useful self-help tool to use as you work to achieve your vision without external pressure. Unfortunately, it is common to compromise, neglect, and sacrifice dreams in order to survive. It is extremely important to carve out the time and resources to give attention to the precise course you want your life to take. In this book you will find ideas on how to focus on details that can easily be missed in the hectic atmosphere in which you function each day.

Rewards take on a variety of forms which surround you daily. Go the extra mile to seek them out and accept their importance. Victories live within the details of your days. Practice giving detailed attention to the minute details, not just the huge and glaring events which occur. Concentrate on battling every temptation to look to others for confirmation of what should be meaningful or expendable with regard to *your* personal happiness.

To get the most benefit from this book, you might need to redefine your definition of exceeding. You may discover your current perception makes you feel like a failure. The reality is that you prevail time and again. Be careful of comparing your accomplishments to those of others, which can lead you to conclude that yours don't meet certain standards.

The "grass is greener on the other side" mentality is not conducive to appreciating all that you have and hold. Every human on the planet has brown, dead grass in some form or another. The concepts and exercises in *Your Purpose in Life is to Win!* are intended to help you identify and celebrate the true riches that are within and around you at all times.

Readers of my memoir, *PTSD and the Undefeated Me*, have asked whether I believe that I have overcome the condition and gained total control over my life. In other words, they wonder if I think I have attained everything this life has to offer. I do not concern myself with "everything". My conviction is to make a conscious decision to *live* every day and go from there, especially after making it through the tragic events in that book.

That decided, I attempt to act upon that choice in whatever form I am able at any given moment. I've learned to remove the shackles of self-defeat and judgment when I fall short. I encourage you to find contentment in working toward reinforcing the foundations for victory that really matter to you, not someone else. Anything I gain above and beyond that is icing on the cake.

I coined the phrase, The Undefeated Me™, to signify that I am a champion every day that I deliberately choose to actively and aggressively <u>live</u>. This requires dynamic participation in the state of being alive. It entails making a continual effort to walk extraordinarily in what you say and do. It includes acceptance of who you are. For me, that is comprised of standing in the assurance that it is more advantageous for me to uplift, rather than tear down, myself or other people.

Does this mean every day of my life is idyllic? No. It translates into a win every day that I stubbornly choose to not give in to detrimental emotions. And I get bonus points for the rounds I get knocked down, in the form of even greater strength and sureness. But I'm never knocked out. To remain unbeatable involves steadily pressing with all my might to keeping crawling my way out of the pit of pity, bitterness, sadness, and anger – time and again. Like you, when I do get up, I expose the chance for my life and the lives of others to become that much more triumphant. In the meantime, I'm happier, more confident, content, and peaceful knowing that I am working and flowing in the purpose for the endowment of life.

Your perspective definitely has bearing on your belief. What you believe you will do; and your actions take the shape of whatever you accept as true and trust. Your choices today included rising from your bed and starting your day. You also chose to read something that will inspire you and add excellence to your state of being.

Most likely, you have cared for yourself or someone you love in one way or another. Your smile, touch, words of wisdom, or wit fell upon someone who desperately needed it, even if they didn't know of or acknowledge that need. These actions are marks of a victor.

Exquisiteness lives in the seemingly mundane moments, so don't take the small things for granted. Instead, unhook yourself from any ties that bind you to negativity. Work consistently to destroy the killers of contentment. Determine to feed yourself a steady diet of self-acceptance and resiliency.

The world is filled with people who exist in a perpetual state of survival only. Sadly, they lose countless moments of true enjoyment. They focus so intently on the struggle that the wonderful feeling that comes with accomplishment eludes their spirit. They are so wrapped up in the tussle that they don't realize when they have won a round and that it's time to celebrate.

Like everyone else, at some point you become hurt or discouraged enough to give up. Then something or someone provides the reason to stay in the contest for its duration. Count your decision to try again as a massive victory. In fact, it is the one that has the most power because it opens the door to your future potential.

Whomever and wherever you are, there is something for you in this book. All you need is an open mind and the conviction that you deserve the best because you are a one-of-a-kind priceless soul. This is a book that meets readers where they are at the present time without the pressure of predefined expectations within a certain timeframe.

You'll learn, or reaffirm, how to accept and

understand that it is perfectly fine to feel challenged, to make blunders, and to lack all the answers. The unrealistic burden of being perfect is then lifted, leaving you free to explore the destinations of your imagination. It boils down to deciding to take an offensive posture and bracing yourself for the inevitable setbacks which will precede your expected comebacks.

Some parts of the book might make you uncomfortable. Well, I felt uneasy when I dug deep into some of my faults and fears in recent years. Then I clung to a life message that reinforced my determination to be true to myself. I shared it in a blog post a couple of years ago.

"Your imperfections, culpabilities, and errors do not equate to failure. They simply mean you are mortal."

I let this simple concept soak through my entire being. The shame, uncertainty, and fright began to fade away. Now I am able to easily move on to doing the work to strengthen my weaknesses as I go forward. I remind myself of this truth often, especially when background chatter from other people attempts to have me question my truths. And each time I overcome or improve, I place a big old happy tick mark in my win column. Being your own advocate is an ongoing process that is definitely worth mastering.

Since you are living anyway, why not spend this time making your personal journey as impactful as possible? For me, the alternatives (which include animosity, envy, antagonism, terror, nastiness, and unforgiveness) breed unnecessary adversity into whatever moments I have left to enjoy my life on earth.

While many real crises are unavoidable, I ignore and remove myself from people and situations that create inconsequential drama. Choosing to deliberately function positively is a selfish delight; one I think everyone deserves. It lets you bask in your personal conquests. Give yourself a chance to be a self-proclaimed champion.

The creation of a plan is not an intent to erase or escape from all unpleasantness and tragic circumstances in the universe. It is not living in a state of total oblivion. That, of course, is impossible. Calamity and misfortune are unavoidable and often uncontrollable.

However, you can build power, character, self-assurance, and a sense of humor (even laughing at yourself) so you stand more calm and fortified in the midst of unfortunate events. And your shine is so much more polished when happiness and fortune come your way. Also, the optimistic unvanquished lifestyle can be very contagious. You will be pleasantly surprised how many people catch what you have and decide to create their own motivated lifestyle.

The book contains practical ideas as well as affirmations to keep you lifted. There are also exercises to do at your own pace. As I wrote this book, its entire purpose was severely tested by serious issues in my personal life. Though I stumbled, I struggled to get back up the minute I was able to continue. I found enrichment and comfort in the words as I wrote them, which pushed me to keep going. I listened to my own advice, and kept writing until it was complete.

Because purpose is personal, only you can fill in the blanks with answers that pertain to your life. I have no doubt that you will build exactly what you need to reap a lifetime of bountiful success. Let's get started!

2 SELF ACCEPTANCE

"How can you maintain genuine relationships with other people if you are an enemy or stranger to yourself? Be your own very best friend. Treasure this honor and guard it accordingly." ~Sheila Kay

One of the first things you do each morning is look in the mirror to prepare for the day ahead. The composition of your face is burned into your memory for a lifetime. You either like, dislike, or are indifferent to your physical appearance. Your opinion of what you look like changes throughout your life. But the reflection does and always will belong to you alone.

Your face expresses to the world who you are and how you are feeling in a thousand different ways. You know it intimately, far more than the proverbial "back of your hand". But let's say that due to some unfortunate event you suddenly go blind. Do you doubt you could describe your features in great detail, if asked?

Of course you could, because you know how you look from top to bottom and from every angle. You know how you look when you are happy, sad, and in or out of good health. You possess a keen awareness of which clothes look best on your body, as well as the subtle and not so subtle changes in your appearance as you age.

What about your inward self? It is human nature to avoid those personal depths that cause pain, humiliation, or anger. Yet there is danger in examining only your superficial characteristics. If someone asked you what is your favorite color, perfume, food, or movie, it would be easy to rattle them off without pause, even though they may change several times. It is wise to be just as informed with regard to your deeper recesses.

A more profound knowledge of who you are is the basis for awareness, approval, and gratitude for everything you represent. No-holds-barred clarity is imperative in the development of an effective and personalized strategy. The more open you are to receiving your totality, the better your chances of ensuring that you take the necessary steps to acquire all that is yours. It is not an overnight project; it takes decades of continuous deliberation and concentration.

Don't you try to learn as much as possible about a close friend or other loved one? Besides knowing how your friend looks, you also know his or her preferences and dislikes. Even beyond that, as a true friend you are willing and eager to absorb as much as possible about their complexities. You listen intently as they pour out their heart. You know the achievements, problems, and mistakes they have made almost as much as your own. In order to communicate to your friend that you care, you ask appropriate questions related to what they share about themselves. Why?

Because you care greatly about the people you love. You want to have enough information to assist them in finding viable solutions to their problems. It is your desire to rejoice when they are happy and sincerely congratulate them on their accomplishments. When they err, you do not mark them as a dreadful human being because you know who they truly are on the inside.

When you disagree or even quarrel, you are confident that one of you will try to reach out for resolution. As a friend, you know enough about their internal makeup to give them sound advice if necessary, even if it goes contrary to what they think. You can keep their confidence and be an advocate on their behalf.

Are you willing to give yourself attention to the same (or greater) degree? Will you treat yourself with the same amount of love, respect, and honesty? If so, you are purposely setting your feet firmly on the path to win.

Spending time honing your gifts and contributions to this world should predominate punishing yourself for imperfection. Treat yourself to the same assistance, kindness, and patience you freely give to others. Doing so will serve to invigorate you and you gain morale. Strive to be your finest comrade and supporter. No human has your back like you do.

Embracing your Good, Bad, and Even the Ugly

I know for a fact it is not easy to explore hidden realities. Yet it is a crucial step toward the mission you plan to accomplish. During this development, you'll uncover countless identifiers. Some will be virtuous, others not so good. Most are simply facts which have no immediate dramatic impact. However, each bit of information will prove to be extremely useful at some point as you progress. So don't discard any new revelations. Wait for the opportunity to utilize what you find.

You've made the commitment to become increasingly acquainted with yourself. Expect judgmental critique from within, and strong opinions one way or the other from other people in all probability. For instance, when I dug deep in the pool of self discovery, the first things that popped to the surface were my impatience, temperament, sensitivity and other characteristics which, at that time, I perceived as flaws.

Rather than focusing my attention on the positive, I went through a phase of unsubstantiated turmoil because I judged myself so harshly. That was a total waste of energy and I soon learned punishing myself serves no real purpose. Admit your shortcomings, push for better, and get on with taking care of business.

During that period of self-degradation, people continued to seek my advice, encouragement, or assistance, as always. I understood that, despite my shortfalls, my words, actions, and inspiration served as lifelines to others at certain times. I've been honored to see lives changed for the better based upon a measure of my input, which added to what they already possessed within themselves. I am, like you, a priceless person – flaws and errors included.

Additionally, I discovered that some things I viewed as deficiencies (such as impatience, temperament, and sensitivity) are demonstrably portions of my personality that enable me to overcome. From this perspective, their merit became clear in my mind. Tempered impatience becomes my enthusiasm to complete tasks correctly and in a timely manner. Measured, mindful temperament transforms into passion and advocacy for injustice. Restrained sensitivity reflects profound empathy and intuitiveness. Positive or negative extremes outside of these parameters is imbalance and needs to be checked.

Shifting perspective does not prevent me from awareness of my liabilities. In fact, I have greater consciousness of when they have become untethered and are taking control. I try to quickly admit when I am wrong.

But now I do recognize that I am not always erroneous. Yet I don't feel the need to explain myself or point out the inaccuracy of other parties each and every time. There's so much to do that a lot of times I just let things pass rather than entertain controversy. For the record, when you are able to do this you are exhibiting controlled power – not weakness.

You can also enhance your peace to a higher level without fear. Accountability for yourself abolishes the threat of delusion. It gives you the power and courage to balance and adjust before things go too far. The act of self monitoring places a buffer between you and intentionally cruel criticism.

Inevitably, you will uncover some things about yourself you dislike, just like you do with friends or family members. Surely you have discovered personality traits in a trusted companion which are contrary to yours. Do you dismiss the relationship or friendship based upon such differences? Do you constantly remind that person of their faults, ignoring their good qualities which make them so dear to you? Your obligation, as your truest and closet friend, is to be as supporting and accepting as possible.

Surround Sound

People will have strong opinions about you and whatever endeavors you choose. There is always a buzz created by voices near you as well as from a distance. Trust yourself to determine which ones to listen to and which to swat away from your earlobe like an annoying insect.

Certainly, you should accept and lean on the people in your life who care for you to their full capacity. You can't succeed credible input from reliable sources. Genuine support serves to fortify your convictions. But if you don't sponsor your own cause, their efforts are useless. In that state you won't take advantage of the prospects their support presents.

Your closest relationships are based upon the mutual actions of both parties. You share secrets (good and bad), ideas, and a variety of life experiences. If your friend makes a mistake, do you allow them to hang their head in shame and mutilate themselves mentally and emotionally? Your first instinct is to encourage that person to do better next time. You tell them about the times you have messed up in a similar manner. To be your own "forever buddy" you must pour yourself out the same benevolence.

Your nearest and dearest meet your needs and wants. Friends care profoundly about what happens to one another. You don't, nor should you, expect flawless devotion, but enough for you to trust them and their motives; they expect the same. You reciprocate by not judging them and firmly supporting their affirmative ideas, hopes, and dreams. Imagine the consequences if you dared to apply all of these principles to the person you see in the mirror!

Do not give yourself the option of disliking who you are as a person. Trust yourself to understand what is appropriate for the undeniable you. Do not question your good motives. Then move forward, being careful not to obsess over your limitations or everything you hear.

Overall, you are a person anyone would be privileged to befriend. Knowing this, you are willing and even eager to share what you have to offer. Soon you will see what others see and appreciate yourself more than anyone else in the world. Think about what you could accomplish, large or small, by being the unquestioning, loyal, funny, and supportive friend to yourself that you are to others.

Copy and Waste

You labor to gather a team made up of people you

respect and who respect you in return. Your innermost circle is comprised of people whom you can inspire and also receive motivation. Useful information is drawn from people you respect and admire. They help you make choices that bolster what you are born to accomplish.

On the other hand, there are those who go beyond admiring other people to downright worshipping them. They see themselves as subservient in one or many ways. Perhaps they see that person as more attractive, smarter, or financially secure. However, you esteem yourself just as high as you do other individuals.

There is nothing at all wrong with good looks, intelligence and stable assets. What poses a real threat is if admiration creates rejection of self and a preference for being someone else.

I call this behavior using another person as a mirror. In other words, looking into a reflection and claiming an image that does not belong to you. It is not you; it is somebody else's looks, life, accomplishments, or blessings. If you know of someone live such a lifestyle, be sure to encourage them to avoid this habit for a myriad of reasons. I know when you think about it you could write your own book of the reasons to be cautious of this to the fullest extent.

External influence is inherent. It starts when children watch and then try to immolate parents, siblings, teachers or others who mold and shape them. It is just as normal for adults be motivated by other people. Exchange of ideas and wise counsel is necessary to boost and guide you forward to the completion of your accomplishments. To aspire to try new notions drawn from someone else is standard, and an effective way to instill freshness to your vision. In turn you influence or mentor others with exceptional results.

What I'm referring to here is another beast entirely. I'm talking about going to mental, emotional, and physical extremes in an attempt to duplicate. It is like a type of 'personality plagiarism'. A person can demonstrate this behavior by constant meticulous, methodical study of every move, expression, talent, or anything else related to their focus.

The intent is "be like" (or to be) the object of adoration. You've seen people who invest more time scrutinizing another than giving attention to themselves. This is a sign that a line may be on the verge of being crossed.

The greatest danger is that, while fixated on someone else, the person is not able to see who and what they are in their own right. They shut the door to discovering all of the wonder and grace they have to offer. Unchecked, this can lead to a miserable and frustrating life.

How tragic for them to never know that all along they held their own abundant and astounding personality. It is similar to walking outdoors while looking down at your mobile phone and running into an electrical pole or other object. Not only embarrassing, but potentially unhealthy to say the least.

The object of worship is most likely not nearly heavyweight as they appear. Often, the other person is confused about their own identity, or may even have a totally skewed perception of themselves and the world. How many unfortunate news stories have been published about famous wealthy, beautiful, and talented people who are entangled in sadness or chaos in their personal lives?

A celebrity or other person who has succeeded in a lifestyle or profession which is similar to your own vision, should indeed pique your interest. You will be moved to research their path to realization in a healthy manner. There is worth in getting information which will benefit you in obtaining the results you seek. However, studying involves learning, not copying to the very letter.

To spend months, or perhaps years, trying to imitate another person is a waste of time, talent and resources. Your goals may not be totally unique from everyone else's, but they should be represented in a way that is distinctively your own. Reach inside for originality and you will create a brand that leads and not follows.

Use Caution When Collaboration

Joining forces with someone is a serious undertaking, be it in a marriage, business, or other partnership. While there are millions of earnest people who are born to buoy others, exercise caution with whom you allow to advise you as you realize your dreams. Sadly, not everyone who volunteers to assist, or says yes to your request for aid, has your best interests in mind.

Follow your instincts. Any and everything that causes you to question whether the person taking you under their wing has the best intentions should be thoroughly investigated. Beware of anyone who confuses *assisting* with *partnering*. Trusted sources will be happy to provide you with background support and give you the spotlight as your ideas come to fruition. And if you do decide to take on a full partner, take extra precaution to ensure you've made the best move.

Don't hesitate for a moment to quickly locate someone else who will be straightforward and loyal. Remember, members of your core crew should be just as happy for your good news as you are, if not more. They will not suddenly abandon you or your project when things are not at their best. Thus, anyone in your group that undermines you may be sending a clue for you to take a closer inspection.

Although sound advice is advantageous, don't risk handing over your power to make essential decisions to someone unless you are utterly free from uncertainty. As you build confidence and trust in yourself, you will also become more self-assured. If a decision you make proves to be off base, you gain valuable experience and the ability to tweak ideas that will result in a better outcome the next time.

Nurturing your established personal relationships is equally key, as those ties will be there to cheer you forward along the way. These people are the ones with staying power, who pick up your broken pieces and form them into wholeness. Likewise, your contributions into their lives is essential. Bonds between you are strengthened due to mutual respect and a team mentality.

Self-Check

Closely study the changes which happen as a result of the fulfillment of your specific realities as a person. Why? To find answers which are relevant to questions about your destination. This also helps you to maintain an accurate assessment of where you are in life at any given time and then build from there. Take scrupulous inventory of your strengths, weaknesses, fears, and insecurities. Then dive into even waters in order to get a precise valuation through no one else's eyes but your own.

Most likely you underestimate the value of your composite self. Don't fear that you are being arrogant when you honestly conclude you have much to add to this world. Be realistic and grab hold of your total self, because nothing you do is a deal breaker between you and your right to win. The terms are defined by your individualism.

Don't Fear the Setbacks

Acceptance of your treasure allows room for you to receive then envelop both your significance and defects correspondingly, because they offer important lessons. After all, you can't beat anything or anyone without first knowing the your weaknesses and those of your opponent. Afterward, you approach ways to improve so that you come out on top. Implementation of what you learned is followed by total conquest.

When a friend hits a rough spot you try your best to make them feel better. You don't hesitate to bring a small token or go visit to offer support. Internalize these instincts to be of service when you are faced with difficulties. Be just as kind to your identity. Use them as opportunities to receive from yourself the finest of pampering and nurturing.

You will become weighed down, disappointed, stuck in a rut, and make bad choices. When it does happen, make haste to get back on your feet at all costs. You know what gives you comfort and hope better than anyone else, so it should not be very difficult to lift your own spirits.

Never give up on yourself. Refute any destructive thoughts or words that only breed depression and bleakness. If you fall into dejection, make it a point to work back to expectation. You will naturally shed some tears or spew out a few choice words out of frustration. Rest in the assurance that the winner in you will rise to sprint toward the finish line yet again.

Proper execution of your plan is your responsibility. However, unless you get a firm grip on who you are, the entire scheme falls apart. If your idea of thorough success came to your door beautifully gift wrapped, how could you recognize and savor it if you didn't know it was meant for you?

How would you know what to do with it if you haven't become skilled at trusting your own persona? If you haven't firmly convinced yourself that you deserve the gift of victory, would you feel it was undeserved and give it away? Would you squander the gift? Knowledge and acceptance of self is the first step. Position yourself to play to win. After all, you are included among the brightest superstars in existence!

Accept what cannot be changed, but make the most of these circumstances by seeking and discovering the positive within them. Use your struggles as weightlifts which add bulk and strength. As for the things that *can* be changed, make the required modifications in your own timing as you go along.

Relish your voyage and the stops along the way. Retain what you're learning, focus on how you're feeling, and celebrate the forward progress. Rely on your value, keeping in mind that it is greater than you can ever imagine. It may not feel that way most of the time; however, feelings are not necessarily facts.

You must recognize that there is a difference between what you *feel* and what is **real**! Resist the urge to compare all that you are and do with anyone else's experience. Doing these things unfailingly is undoubtedly difficult, but the return on the investment is nothing short of amazing.

SELF ACCEPTANCE

In chapter two you laid a mental foundation to begin your expedition. You considered the possibilities and advantages of being your most loyal defender and advocate. These exercises will encourage you to hold tight to the concepts and strive for discovering what works to help you beat all odds. Keep a notebook or create a computer file to complete the exercises in this book.

- Write down a few activities in which you participate that you dislike or feel indifferent about, but only do out of habit or external pressure. Contemplate whether you can eliminate one or more of them in order to spend that time and energy on yourself.

- What types of people do you like/admire/are entertained by/love/or mentor? Are you willing to edit your circle so that it is only inhabited with people who meet these criteria, or any other reasons you find necessary?

- Take note of five things or attributes that you know you look good in or excel in doing. They can include clothes or jewelry, etc. Or your list can consist of traits like humility, generosity, humor, and the like. Stop writing after the first five that pop in your mind. Then quiet your mind and congratulate yourself fully. For the next week, showcase the items on the list in ways such as what you wear, speak and do. Ignore any negativity from within yourself or others. Repeat the same exercise each week, adding as many as possible during each session. You're incorporating solid confidence into your plan!

- Don't hesitate to admire yourself and the results of your tenacious efforts. As you go forward, you will see how poise and self-assuredness are vital components you will need to stay strong. There are differences between having humble esteem and being obnoxious or self-centered. In your quest to rise above, you sincerely desire to promote positivity, not drag nasty competition or deliberate contention into your right.

3 YOU ARE WHAT YOU DO

"It may surprise you to discover how many things you do well that you actually dislike doing." ~Sheila Kay

By the end of this chapter you will identify things in your life which you were probably born to do. You will explore past, present, and future endeavors in which you've participated. It will be interesting and fun to uncover the activities in which you participate but don't necessarily like, after all.

There are an abundance daily tasks with which you are charged that much be completed - without option and no questions asked. Allow me to be clear: Success is not luxury to do only makes you happy on some level. In fact, a frontrunner knows that the best part of life is the sacrifice of giving to others. This chapter refers to what you do solely for reasons such as guilt, fear, abuse, or boredom. You may find that quite a few of your undertakings are mere habits that contribute nothing to your life except take up precious time.

Let me share my roast beef story as an example. My mother taught me to cook when I was very young. I

39

enjoyed cooking as a child and caught on very quickly. One dish that I had trouble with was roast beef. Although my roast beef was tasty, I could not seem to get mine to taste as delicious and tender as my mother's for a long time. Fast forward at least 25 years. After much, practice, I regularly place a moist, well seasoned, and tender roast beef on the table.

One evening when I sat down to eat, it occurred to me I didn't even really like roast beef! I watched my husband as he ate and complimented me on the dinner. Although I knew the meal was tasty, I was curious. I asked him to tell me the truth. "Do you really like roast beef?"

You guessed it. He wasn't crazy about roast beef either. All those years of trying to master the dish and I never realized that it wasn't one of his favorites because he ate so heartily. There was nothing wrong with the taste; it was simply a dish he too could do without.

Of course, I ceased cooking roast beef for Sunday dinner from that point. Why did I work so hard all those years to perfect that dish? For several reasons, I think.

I do believe that the smell of my mother's roast beef brought me comfort growing up. So maybe I was trying to impart the same feeling to my family. Also, I am most comfortable when things are done properly, period. I don't stop trying until I am satisfied something is as close to my version of flawless as possible. I am an undiagnosed, but self-proclaimed, obsessive perfectionist. I still make a delicious roast beef. For other people.

You too may excel at something but not really enjoy the results of the activity. I wonder whether I pressed so hard because I wanted to please my mother. Or, was I telling myself that my perfectly fine roast beef was not good enough? There are a lot of reasons humans continue down a certain path without questioning why.

I shared a real life example of expending talent and time that could have been used more productively elsewhere. Not to say your life isn't filled with things you do for others on a regular basis. But I'm sure you get the point. People can easily find themselves in a repetitive rut doing expendable activities, sometimes for a lifetime.

All deeds you do basically extend from your natural personality, interests, and talents. In the roast beef example, I would say that my love of family, persistence in perfection, and interest in cooking well are elements of what kept me engaged for so long learning to cook roast beef with excellence. But in the end it was something I could discontinue without causing harm, leaving room to pursue other interests. However, my cooking talents and business sense combined and let me to open a catering company later in life.

The importance of getting to know yourself includes a genuine familiarity with your real personality traits, which saves time, money, headache, and heartache. To the extent possible, line up your pursuits with your personality, then add in something that challenges you.

Have you ever encountered a customer service person who looked and behaved as if they were miserable or angry? This type of person refuses to smile, make eye contact, or say thank you - no matter how pleasant you are towards them.

Sure, anyone can have a bad day. But have you gone to the same store on another day and been served by the same person behaving in the identical manner? There could be a number of causes for their behavior. For instance, the person is not sociable whatsoever, an illness, or he/she is better suited for other employment or purpose.

That's the beauty of an efficacious life. With true commitment and hard work, you can rearrange certain parts of your life. Be willing to be comfortable with reaching beyond your present situation for the what is ideal for you and the legacy you leave behind.

If the cause of the attitude of the customer service person in the example above is unhappiness with their job, they could instead plan ahead. In time they could consider self employment, work from home, or perform work that does not require social interaction. This same individual could excel in a new environment. I'll sum it up in three words: Explore your options. Making a firm decision to move away from what makes you miserable is a good place to start.

There is no magic wand that will solve life's problems, but you know that already. But a fierce, made up mind changes negatives into positives. You possess a catalogue of characteristics which, if used properly, will place you at the front of the line every time.

Continue getting to know the various aspects of your personality, and don't panic when you see how many traits are rolled up into the person you've become. Remember, they can and should be configured for constructive change. Do you know someone who is very sensitive, arrogant, analytical, and generous, yet extremely cautious, almost appearing to be paranoid?

At first glance this seems like a strange mixture in a personality profile, doesn't it? And it can be, if such a person chose a career and hobbies in which they are incompatible or disinterested. But a person with these very traits would also make a great attorney, surgeon, minister, or any number of other professions. What other occupations can you think of that could benefit from having someone like this on the payroll?

What You Were Created to Be (or Not to Be)

If you are gifted in, and have real passion for, what you do for a living, consider yourself a winner in this regard no matter the amount of your salary. Doing what you love and getting paid for it is a fantasy come true. Those who have achieved this objective also have the freedom to engage in a wide variety of other interests and activities in addition to their career. Many of them spend time teaching, mentoring, training, and supporting other people who have the same or similar aspirations.

The majority of people in the world are employed in jobs they don't necessarily love in order to afford the necessities of life. Many retire after decades of successful, if not fulfilling, employment. Are they not unbeatable go-getters? Of course they are! They are who this country is made of and deserve all the respect it can offer for their commitment to support their families before anything else they do.

Though the average worker does not report to their ideal job each day, in all likelihood they have talent, education, and the personality (or all of these) that are compatible with what they do. Otherwise, it would be next to impossible to stay in, perform, or even surpass others in their field.

Millions of people choose the security of a steady job even as they pursue their dream career. They balance out their creative side by engaging in compatible hobbies, entertainment, or volunteer work. Some even enroll in classes to earn a degree in a field they would enjoy working in the future. So many possibilities exist in life to make yours noteworthy.

What's The Difference?

The importance of coming to terms with and

embracing your exceptional personality was also discussed in the second chapter. However, contentment and gain are unlikely if you do not really have a handle on what are your talents, gifts, and interests, too. All of these work in tandem to be utilized to the fullest.

For you to walk in your richness you must identify these three components. Just as important, you have to know their differences. Knowledge of all planes of **who you are** is a chief component of your purposed life plan.

Gifts and talents are frequently interchangeable. They both refer to things that you can do with minimal effort. Usually, they involve enterprises in which you take delight. Your gifts and talents are easy to identify because they most always lend themselves to a part of your personality. You flow in them with ease and grace.

There are a couple of small variances between talents and gifts. Innate, or natural, gifts require less study or preparation and practice to perform efficiently. Inborn gifts are harder to lose sight of than talents. Even if they haven't been used in a while, it is easier to exercise such a gift than to quickly pick up again with a learned interest after a period of inactivity. Gifts last a lifetime with little exception.

Talents, whether natural or learned, do take more practice to become proficient. Without continued maintenance, it is possible to permanently lose a talent over time. For instance, athletes and musicians are both gifted and talented. But it is imperative that they practice/rehearse regularly in order to remain in and excel in their field.

Like talents, gifts also need to be nurtured. Continued education, participation, and staying on top of the latest news and information are just a few ways to keep gifts and talents in top form. Both can be used for self and/or to benefit someone else. All three usually run in families, sometimes spanning several generations.

Interests include unexplored subjects, people, or activities. You can easily identify an interest because, more likely than not, you find yourself reading, researching, or thinking and talking about a particular topic over others. Sometimes your intense curiosity begins suddenly. You are drawn to the subject but may have not had time, opportunity, or resources to explore further.

Interests are infinite in range, from lifelong dreams to a newfound inquisitiveness. With time and effort, a new interest becomes a lifelong gift or talent; even if it is something in which you have not had prior participation. Your personality, gifts, talents, and interests are all expressed through the type of employment, hobby, charitable work, lifestyle preferences, and other avenues within your life you choose.

Place the same amount of effort in learning what *is not* a personal fit for you. Constantly chasing after ventures in which you will most likely be unsuccessful, or won't enjoy, is sabotage. Take your time making choices so you can follow up on what you do discover within without apprehension.

Make targeted choices, but remain flexible. Take a career in sports, for instance. Maybe you don't honestly have natural athletic ability, but it is your sincere desire to work in that vocation. Consider exploring a career in sports physical therapy, coaching, business management, or consulting as alternatives to participating in the sport and risking injury or disappointment. Give this part of the process ample time to develop fully as you accept your decision to compromise, if necessary. Be patient. You are still travelling in the right direction.

Gradually, you will acknowledge your true motives for investigating or continuing in an activity, career or relationship. Chapter two also emphasized the significance of being your best friend. Therefore, do not judge your reasons; admit and consent to honest answers about your incentives.

Let's say you conclude that your motives are financially motivated. Then focus on what you should do to facilitate ways to make as much profit as possible. Among dozens of other motivations are community enrichment, notoriety, spiritual fortification, service to others, and family matters.

You may find you have several motives. Give each positive intention equal validity. Push even harder to reveal them, starting with the strongest incentive. Now you're creating that roadmap to elation with less detours, confusion and procrastination.

At some point in time, everyone has to complete tasks totally unrelated to reaching an ultimate life goal – or so it may seem. Some of these tasks are taking care of a sick or elderly family member, managing finances, and housework, to name a few. They seem as if they are worlds apart from what you envision success to look like. However, your consistent performance to the best of your ability means that you are responsible and dependable.

These characteristics are the most valuable personal assets to own, whatever your future holds.

Once your responsibilities are complete, your mind is cleared for the exploration phase of your plan. Outside of these obligations there is some time to dedicate to your dream life. You can concentrate on trimming the fat, so to speak, of activities and people which may hinder your vision.

You Can Have It All

Is it possible to be content in life while juggling the necessities with enjoyable, profitable, and self-fulfilling pursuits? Yes, take advantage of your ability to adjust. You can tip the scales in your favor by deliberately arranging your priorities and making thoughtful choices each day.

These are some of the tools that create chances for you to satisfy your desire to get ahead:

1. Time management
2. Patience
3. Honesty
4. Careful decision making
5. Humility
6. A sincere support system

7. Self love

8. Creativity and imagination

9. Determination

10. Focus

A Few Things to Remember

It's almost impossible to become an expert at anything without consistent upkeep and usage. Stay on top of the latest information about your gift, talent, or interest. Information changes with the passage of time.

If you take notice of something brand new and believe it is compatible with your goals, take small steps in that direction to see where it leads. Don't give up on the interest (or invest a lot of time pursuing it) until you are fully convinced whether it is for you or not.

Be very careful about forcing a fit. Trust yourself and your instincts enough to follow what you feel that you are called to do. In the early stages, it is normal for everything not to fall perfectly in place. You can amend later. But after time, if you realize you have to stop giving time, money, and effort to the cause, be bold enough to cut your losses. There will be plenty of signs to show you that you won't get the results you deserve.

At the same time, avoid placing restrictions, such as time limits, on creating and executing your course of action. Remain mindful that your personality, talents, and gifts will eventually get you where you need to be on your path. It is a balancing act that you can definitely master and execute if you concentrate and prepare in advance.

YOU ARE WHAT YOU DO

Be as open and genuine as possible in your answers and assessments. If you don't know the answers right now, that is normal. It is an asset that you have the patience to wait and consider carefully before answering.

Expect your answers to change as you grow. There are no wrong or right answers, judgment, or competition. This is a fact finding assignment. Revise your discoveries as it becomes necessary.

- Determine how much extra time you have each week outside of necessary responsibilities. List the top 3 ways you spend that spare time (outside of work and business or family obligations). If you conclude you have no spare time, now is the time to get creative and squeeze out a couple of hours a week at a minimum.

- Begin a separate list of activities, people, or other things you can cut out or reduce to make room for targeted progress toward completing your mission.

- Write or type your immediate reaction (as of today) to the following scenarios. Your answers will give insight into your personality and character.

    1) You have worked hard for several months on a project that is important to you. You expect by now to see results which reward your work and justify the time you spent. So far it has yielded no results or recognition. Today, you have a strong urge to give up.

    2) You excel in a certain gift, talent, or interest to such a degree that you start a successful business venture. After a year, you discover someone else has started a business very similar to yours. It seems to be prospering and it is near your location.

    3) A friend you have trusted for many years has been exposed as disloyal and backbiting to not just you, but all of his/her friends and associates. You have

few other close friends. The two of you have shared everything - money, secrets, fun times. You have confirmed the disloyalty.

- Start a list with four columns which represent what you believe are your personality traits, gifts, talents, and interests. Add an item to each column. Keep the list and add or subtract often.

4 RELATIONSHIP PROXIMITY

"There are people in your life who are so close to you that they are almost like your second skin. If someone in your inner circle consistently causes you harm in any way, you may have to behave like a snake. Shed them and then leave them behind." ~Sheila Kay

Even a self-proclaimed "loner" is obligated to interact with other people in some fashion. It may be with family members, co-workers, neighbors, or friends. This chapter covers a variety of relationships. It will help you identify and categorize the people in your life and their proximity to your core. An accurate assessment of the relationships between those that surround you is definitely in your best interests.

Here is a basic list of categories of people with whom you network. There are probably those in your life that fit into more than one category.

- Immediate family (spouse, parents, children, siblings, etc.)
- Other family members (in-laws, cousins, etc.)
- Close friends (friends you connect with regularly)

- Acquaintances (people you interact with on a limited basis)
- Colleagues/Classmates
- Community/recreational (church members, leisure activity teammates, neighbors)
- Social media connections
- New people (someone just you've met and are deciding where they fit in your life)

In the statement above I compared those closest to you with the skin on a snake. I was referring to people you know that do not contribute to the betterment of your life. Chief among these are individuals who go even further by intentionally attempt to destroy others every chance their given. If such a person has a tent in your camp, you may find it necessary to examine your options with regard to severing the tie.

Of course, you do have personalities in your life that you cannot walk away from for various reasons, such as close family members. Shedding, in this instance, does not mean walking away forever, or not loving them. But perhaps you can love from a physical or emotional distance if they consistently tear at the fabric of your peace and contentment.

This decision shouldn't be taken lightly. It should come after you have attempted to find peace with the relative, especially one that is in close proximity. Your mind should be at ease, without concern that you have misunderstood their intentions, or that you are having a sensitive moment from which you will recover. It is detrimental to try to turn other relatives against this person. Rather, let them make their choice based upon their own interactions with the relative.

Do not become obsessed about the situation; just determine that you will remain firm in following your peaceful purpose. Love them; do not let their shortcomings cause you to become bitter. This means to wish them the best in their own lives without becoming caught up in their drama. To love from a distance also means that you do no harm to them in word or in deed. True forgiveness, in some cases, can only come when you are distanced from the cause of your hurt. Be mindful that there is a possibility that one day the two of you can reconcile differences. Try not to harden your heart permanently as you sit on the other side of your wall of protection.

Prepare your heart and mind to accept that the decision you made is life changing. It isn't easy to make the decision to distance yourself from a harmful relative. You may feel guilty and second guess the motives of the offender. You might question your interpretation of what was said or done. Or you may feel pressure from other relatives who disagree with your choice. For the sake of your own harmony and balance, it may be inevitable, even if only for a season to give yourself time to heal before reconciling. If you have consistently been hurt, discouraged, or angry when in the presence of a relative, it is probably a red flag to tell you it is best to take action for both of your sakes.

It is possible to guard yourself even if circumstances place you in the same physical location. How? Make a conscious decision to not react if they attempt to push buttons or engage you in negativity. Limit one-on-one time with them as much as possible if you sense there is still angst between you.

But be firm in your conviction not to allow any of their venom to invade your system. One of the reasons that snakes shed their skin is so that parasites which attach to their skin are removed and left behind.

Did you know that snakes also shed their skin so they can grow? One reward you reap by shedding "dead skin" is that you open up the opportunities for maturity and growth. Meet new people and forge healthy relationships, if you so desire. Use the energy you formerly used in toxic relationships to uncover ways to fortify your winning way of living.

No Kin of Yours

The decision to release people who are not blood related is easier, isn't it? Maybe; but this is another area that depends solely on the individual. For instance, you may be a person who nurtures very close ties to friends. Your friendships are knit together as closely as those in your family. But the same principle applies; if any bond is damaging to you, it is wise to develop an exit strategy.

What are some of the signs that a friend or other acquaintance is a threat to your serene existence? Most likely, your instinct will lead you to discover that you feel less confident, unhappy, and discontent after interacting with that person. There is a reason for these feelings. If you find yourself on the defensive more often than not, give the relationship some attention. It could be that a connection has run its course. After all, it is possible for people to grow apart after time. Hopefully, the issue is miscommunication that can be straightened out. But if not, don't force any affiliation.

Maybe what brought you together is no longer relevant to you or the other person. It could be as simple as your differences over time have made you incompatible. Naturally, in a true relationship these reasons are not in and of themselves a cause to shut down all operations. But you will know whether that is the plausible option based upon how you and the other person relate to one another on a consistent basis.

By far, most of the people who have made it into your inner circle are true to your team and the course it is following. They stand behind you in positive support. Each of you is free to express independent opinions and life choices without hurt feelings or resentment. You walk away feeling validated and strengthened, never depressed or insecure. These are the connections that have staying power. Time, circumstances, or distance have no negative effect on such a linking. Continue to fight to keep these valuable people in your life.

Almost everyone has someone that is considered a friend, but in reality there is no real loyalty between the two. They are known as "frenemies", a dangerous mixture of friendship and contention, jealousy, competition, or other negative undertones. Yet for some reason it is nearly impossible to extricate yourself from this type of contrary relationship. Deep inside you know that it does not add substance to your existence, but the two of you have become too comfortable with the dysfunction and are convinced that a real friendship exists.

You are learning to look closer into why you do the things that you do; here is another area that calls for introspection. Ask yourself why you do not remove yourself from such a love/hate cycle. There is no right or wrong answer, but you must be honest about your reasons. Do either or both of you remain close because of money, affection, or loneliness? Do you remain in the friendship because you enjoy being a "frenemy" yourself? Are you afraid this person, or using the person to make other connections from which you can benefit? Ask yourself the hard questions and be prepared for answers which may surprise you.

It could also be that the two of you are co-dependent or have become accustomed to less than genuine friendship. Quality will always trump quantity. So don't hesitate to break free, even if it means that you have a limited number of real friends.

Do not criticize yourself about your reasons for staying, or for the time you spent in such a friendship or other relationship. Now is not the time for beating up on yourself. This is a time of seeing things clearly, of self-acceptance, and being brave enough to make beneficial changes. You are in the midst of being deliberate in everything you do. This moment in your life has been given you to surround yourself with class in every area of your life.

Just like with family, there are people with whom you must have contact for one reason or another. Examples include co-workers, classmates, and neighbors. Most likely, they are not as close to you as relatives or close friends. Even so, recognize that they can still have an impact on your overall peace in some manner. The choice is yours; either become drawn into contentiousness or spend the least amount of time together. Place distance between you and their pessimism.

You can walk in your purpose of peace by avoiding confrontation and remaining calm whenever you are forced to be in the presence of a consistently divergent individual. Also, make sure you do not allow others to pull you into disparaging conversation involving the other party. As the saying goes, "Be careful of the dog that brings you the bone". Watch out for anyone who insists on telling you what the other person said or did; there's usually a reason for their interest in your discord between the two of you.

The popularity of the Internet and social media makes it necessary to address associations in these arenas. It is currently possible to make cyber friends (and enemies) from anywhere on the planet. Online networking can be helpful for your business or social life. How closely do you allow people that you have never met (and may never meet in person) to get to your distinct real life essence? Should you devote the time and energy to these acquaintances that you do to in person relationships? It is entirely your choice.

If you do closely connect with friends on the Internet, the same rules apply. Examine the relationship, focusing on how it makes you feel overall. Do you turn off the computer feeling rejected, angry, or defensive? Rather than exposing yourself to unhealthy energy, consider using the block feature.

To engage in retaliation or defend yourself against someone who has obviously made up his/her mind is pointless and inefficient. Hopefully, you have made healthy connections among the millions of people online. And it is into those friendships that you make regular deposits.

If you have found it necessary to put distance between you and other people in your life, what do you do with the void (large or small) that is left after their departure? It takes knowing yourself intimately to decide. You have many options from which to choose. You may decide to leave the void empty of people and fill it with pursuing your passions. Then again, you could open yourself up to explore relationships with new people that you meet on your journey.

These same concepts also apply to new people you meet. Take note of the mutual, or potential, benefit of forming a relationship. Foster value and loyalty. Reject destructive behavior at any level. Whether you decide not to fill the space or find new friendships depends on you alone. The beauty is that you can do both.

Doing Your Part in Relationship Success

Just as important is that you supply a regular outpouring of support into your valuable relationships. Make concessions in what you think, say, and do for the good of the union. Develop a routine of looking in the mirror to make sure you have the reflection of a loyal friend.

I "clutched the pearls" in shock, so to speak, when I dared to face the fact that I could be selfish sometimes. Who me? Sheila 'give the shirt off my back' Kay? But my stinginess had nothing to do with material things. Mine is of a more emotional nature.

For instance, I sometimes develop tunnel vision when I am working on a project and tend to pull away from those closest to me, mentally and physically. Or, if I am really struggling, I tend to go inside myself like a turtle to his shell. I have accepted my shortcomings and that the world doesn't stop when I am up to my neck in tasks or not feeling my best. People still do need me to be available to some degree, so I do my best to give attention to those I love even when I am busy. I am more likely to explain why I need space rather than exit silently.

Family and friends don't always need tangible things. And there are occasions when they don't even want unsolicited advice. Instead, try to be aware of times when all that is needed is your undivided attention. Very often, a patient listening ear is just the ticket to turn their bad day into one with a better ending. I have learned to accept that am I am not created to fix everything. Even more humbling, I have not, and never will, be able to do so.

So as you work through defining and prioritizing your relationships, don't forget to check to see whether you are doing your best to be just as deserving as the person on the other side.

Points to Ponder

As humans, we shed our physical skin during an ongoing and unconscious process over the course of our lives. This is done naturally, without fanfare or notice. Snakes slough off their skin in one piece - like removing an article of clothing. From that point they are free to grow and explore the next phase of their lives as the new layer of skin grows. This can be compared to humans who choose to leave behind parasites in the form of destructive people, words, and behavior to pursue possibilities beyond their dreams.

Interestingly, snakes also prepare ahead of time for renewal of their skin. They swim in water to help loosen the old skin. They rip the old skin, (usually near the mouth, by the way), to facilitate its removal. Snakes rub against rough objects like rocks or logs to help get rid of skin that has passed the time of usefulness. You too can prepare yourself for any relationship changes that may be overdue. Start with following your instincts that tell you a relationship is harmful. Then prepare your heart and mind for the changes in your life that will occur if you do, indeed, find it necessary to break away.

A snake removes itself from the old skin inch by inch. Therefore, it is possible to see a snake that is inside out because the shedding is incomplete. There will be times when you feel this way. You will be out of sorts, confused, and maybe even lonely after you decide the best course is to pull apart from someone. Don't let these feelings deter you from staying on your path.

Finally, like the snake, make it a regular habit of evaluating and reevaluating your relationships. Snakes shed their skin between two to four times each year on average. But younger snakes, which are in the actively growing time of their lives, do so about every two weeks. So it is with you. As you implement your plan, increase the number of times you take assessment of those that surround you. The end result will leave you with more stable and less volatile associations that are favorable to your ambitions.

RELATIONSHIP PROXIMITY

Work through these exercises gradually. Expect the effort to be complicated and difficult at times. You will no doubt have setbacks as you attempt to apply these lessons in your life. Remember, keep your concentration on the life you are building. Start over as often as necessary.

- Begin the process of purposeful association. Fine tune your instincts regarding people whose motives seem questionable. Refrain from making changes until you are sure they are warranted, not that you are simply having a paranoid moment or in a bad mood.

- Don't be in a hurry to end relationships that may turn out to be salvageable. As it is said, "Give a person enough rope and they will hang themselves." Be watchful but fair. If someone is not good for you, it will be clearly revealed in time.

- Be careful not to internalize how people make you feel or take revenge upon the wrongdoer. Recognize that you are hurting, but do not give in to the temptation to repay evil for evil. To do so would be to emulate the behavior of the other party, which is contrary to who you plan to be in life.

- Within one week of reading this chapter, choose at least one of the most loyal and dear people in your circle. Reach out and make firm plans to spend quality time together. A token of appreciation, an outing, or just some great conversation will be good for you both. It is also a great investment into a deserving relationship.

5 MIND CONTROL

"One day I heard someone bullying, threatening and insulting me. They questioned by abilities and my motives for actions that I take. I felt angry, confused, and hopeless. I listened more closely to determine who dared attempt to destroy me with such malicious criticism and spiteful lies! I was shocked when I realized the voice was my own."
~Sheila Kay

"What are you thinking about"? Certainly, you've asked and have been asked that question countless times. A happy, sad, angry, or other facial expression usually prompts this query. That is because what humans are thinking in their mind almost always shows in their countenance and/or posture. Then it slides off your face and steps into your life in the form of action.

In this chapter you will be encouraged remain to cognizant of what occupies your mind most frequently. You will discover that you can control what you think by making a conscious effort to change adverse thoughts briskly and often. You have the ability to shut out unproductive or destructive thoughts and replace them with your aspirations.

This chapter is not a medical, philosophical or spiritual lesson. It does offer reminders, practical suggestions, and examples of making sound choices regarding your mindset. These can result in an improvement in how you view yourself and the world in general.

Only the most narcissistic or delusional person can totally avoid invasive negative thoughts. It is next to impossible to have a mind filled with blissful images and sunlight twenty-four hours a day – at least once you live past two years of age. But without intervention, a darkened mindset can become a runaway train that leads to mental (and in some cases physical) derailment.

You can put your mind in check as soon as you recognize a pattern of hazardous thinking. Purposely turn away from intense guilt or self-blame each time they surface. Challenge all forms of intense pressure, unfair criticism, and harsh judgment. Don't assume that this kind of imbalanced thinking is always true. Act before such distortions take root in your mind and you start to view them as facts. Because before you know it, you will follow the direction your thoughts take you.

There are ways to counteract mental demons, though tough discipline is required. They include:

- Understand that what you think affects you physically. Take note of the thoughts you have and ascertain whether they are helpful or harmful to your body.

- Correct any perceptions that you know are harmful. For instance, if a thought such as "I am worthless" pops in your head, quickly replace the space it takes up in your mind with something like "(fill in the blank) loves and needs me", or "I do (fill in the blank) very well".

- During the times you find your mind is stagnant, focusing solely on the unfavorable, get to work. Fight your way out by identifying the untruths and writing down or speaking the advantages of shaking off ugliness. Refuse to give negativity power over you. Give the comfort of loving compassion to the best friend you are becoming to yourself.

Self-love is not a fabrication that you are perfect and blameless. In fact, accept you have flaws and seek areas of improvement during your self-discovery. Just as you have repairs made to an automobile or home, correcting yourself is a form of taking pride in ownership.

But a mind filled with uninhibited toxins can kill anything and everything you possess. It can turn winners into losers, victors into failures, and the healthy into deathly sick. No doubt you have heard the expression, 'the battlefield is in the mind'. It is true. Whatever fight you face has deep roots in the cerebral.

The brain is where you start to gather (or surrender) your **weapons**, formulate **strategies** for combat (or become complacent), and **fight** with all of your might (or admit defeat). You have the power to choose your weapons and to use them. You take command of how you feel by what you think. You possess the ability to defend yourself against the inevitable fear, discouragement, and insecurity that creep in your mind.

Let's take each of these points and throw out a few examples of what they are and how to use them.

Weapons	Strategies	Active Combat
Awareness that you may be thinking negatively even when you don't realize it.	**Decide** to make pursuit of a quality mindset a lifetime priority.	**Guard** what goes into your mind by being careful what you see, say, and hear.
Determination to consciously and consistently change unhealthy thought patterns.	**Create** an effective strategy to manage your thoughts each day.	**Strike** back by replacing dangerous thoughts.
Support from friends, family and other sources.	**Resolve** to refresh your mind and start over as many times as needed.	**Study** the enemies of your mind so that you recognize when and how they try to attack.

Incorporate these guidelines into the part of your prosperity objective which relate to a healthy mental status. Don't be misled into thinking that you are exempt from mental attack. You will add your own elements as you become more in tune with what goes on in your own head. For instance, you may realize that certain situations or people trigger thoughts that endanger you. In time, you will learn to avoid engaging in thoughts for long periods of time which only lead you to a dead end with no productivity.

But what if you are faced with a monumental situation that you cannot control? In all truth, there is no real answer, only suggestions that may help to ease the impact to some small degree. In the majority of unplanned, unexpected trials in life, your fight is not the situation itself. The real foe is the struggle against giving in to hopelessness and depression. I cannot think of an assault more difficult than this sort, because it is usually combined with some type of loss.

Unfortunately, there is no way to avoid thinking about a tragedy, trauma, or other crisis. Even so, with time and attention, it is possible to replace the most painful of thoughts or, at a minimum, distract your mind until the most awful periods pass. The worst thing you can do is chastise yourself for whatever reaction you may be having during this time. Keep reminding yourself that there will be better times on the other side of the agony. Acknowledge that our only option is to reach that point at your own pace.

Who? Me?

What if you discover that it is you who tends to be your most dangerous enemy? Do not let this shock you. In fact, most people take on the role of their own saboteur a time or two in their lives. There are countless reasons for this, including environment, trauma, genetics, and more.

You should consider this as a possibility. However, it does not mean that you are free to accept it as a permanent way of life. Instead, you absolutely must affirm your worth by fighting for better and greater. Victory, in all shapes and sizes, should be your state of mind and way of life.

The flip side to this revelation is that you are the easiest enemy to defeat in your fight for a winning life. One advantage is that, even when you're feeling bad about yourself, by nature it is not so easy to do yourself any real harm.

You also have the advantage because you know yourself more intimately than anyone else. Knowing your opponent is a key to victory, as you well know. So figuring out what would make you turn your thinking around is not an insurmountable task. Use that knowledge to challenge the lies you tell yourself. Are there life changes that would make you happier about who you are? Is there someone in your life with whom you should make peace?

Sometimes a negative mindset is the result of boredom, or loneliness, or being afraid. It could be a physical reason, such as your blood sugar is low and you need to eat. Search for a reason why you are being unkind to your best friend in the whole world.

When I wrestle with my mind, I say aloud, "You are alright Sheila. Nothing's wrong." And I can't tell you how many times I literally say "Stop!" out loud when my mind wants to turn left toward discouragement or despair. And I am not ashamed; rather, I am proud to share these truths. They increase my authority and power over defeatism. I've lived each word I've written in this book. Hopefully, they serve to help you in some way.

You see, I stand in the midst of a challenging contest that I'm resolute to win because the prize is my very life. And so do you. Take action immediately to pull away from self-abuse through undesirable thinking. Whatever the case, don't keep hurting your own feelings.

I suppose you know already that there are other people who are all too happy to keep you on the defensive. Some of these unfortunate individuals attempt to make you insecure or salivate at the thought of inflicting pain. People who know me have heard me say countless times that it isn't always what people say that hurts. A lot of times it's what they *don't* say. Sometimes that silence is filled with derision.

In a nutshell, don't let people get into your head because they have no other purpose than to over-analyze what you do and say. Or they place the greatest urgency upon letting you know they are deliberately ignoring you or your accomplishments. This is another situation in which I don't need to explain to you how to handle. You know what to do. Do it. With a smile on your face.

Refuse to harbor grudges or fury in your mind. Dismiss jealousy, prejudice, resentment and bitterness when they try to curl up inside your soul. Guard against engaging in hurtful conversations about other people. Can you do all of this with a snap of a finger? No. But pushing cynicism in any form from your mind can and should be at the top of your to-do list each day so that it stays sharp and uncluttered.

There is so much at stake on the front line that is your mind. Without a definite plan to control your thoughts, your entire life can be shut down, because you are unable to recover from the beating your brain has taken. If you do nothing and let twisted thoughts run rampant, your reality becomes skewed and you accept less than you should.

Stand your ground against a deadly point of view. Refocus whenever you can for an overall upgraded attitude. You will be more open to try progressive new experiences. Careful practice will soon make it easier for you to act upon productive ideas that your mind conceives.

Not many people can make their mind go totally blank for any length of time. You will always think of something or someone. Choose to make it a point to keep your mental channel tuned in to the finest in your life.

"Living and dreaming are two different things- but you can't do one without the other."

-Malcolm Forbes

MIND CONTROL

The following is an ongoing exercise for you to repeat as often as you wish to manage your inner voice. Take your time going through each step.

1. Periodically, write down five things that you have thought about yourself. Separate these thoughts into negative and positive. Categorize if the thought relates to your past, present, or your future, if applicable.

2. Read them aloud as if someone else was talking to you. Take a moment between each one to process what you feel. Write down your emotional and physical reaction.

3. Count the numbers of each type of thought to get an idea of how negatively or positively you view yourself as a whole.

4. Write an affirmative statement for every negative thought.

5. Read the affirming statement aloud. Tune in to what you feel emotionally and physically and take notes.

6 ENVIRONMENT

"Your environment is an integral part of your overall happiness. It is one of few areas of life that you have the ability to manage, and you must do so for your greater good." ~Sheila Kay

Ask any group of people what is happiness, and you'll get a wide spectrum of answers. Like snowflakes, happiness is shaped, matchlessly, for each individual; it is exclusive. Happiness evokes images full of eternal sweetness and light, which is why a lot people doubt its existence. However, it is filled with complexities which even the recipient cannot fully comprehend.

In this context, it is assumed that you believe in and strive for joy, peace, and contentment. Thus far, you have read how to increase and create opportunities which will compliment your desire to win across the board. Introspection, love of self, your activities, and the people you engage with, are among the areas which can be governed for you to operate at your full potential. This chapter will cover yet another area which has impact upon your satisfaction. It is something over which you can regulate to some degree; namely, your environment.

The powerful effect your environment has on you can be either undesirable or constructive. Let's say you own a multitude of elements which represent success, such as money, fame, family, good health, and expensive material possessions. However, placed in the wrong environment, any and all symbols of prosperity can be systematically destroyed or lost. Your environment, wherever it may be, can be molded and shaped; its core can be carried wherever you go, similar to giving and receiving love.

But nothing that you hold dear can survive a consistently toxic atmosphere. This statement has nothing to do with the appearance of, or objects within, your home. The unhealthy consequences may start off subtly, but eventually your senses absorb what they are exposed to, wherever your location. To the extreme, you will be faced with either accepting inferiority, ignoring that serious problems do exist, or removing yourself from emotional or physical harm.

There is a potential for danger even in the confines of your own home. I cannot stress the extent to which your backdrop influences what you do and how you feel. Again, you have the power to orchestrate this part of your life in several ways.

Your Living Space

Where you live should capture your detailed and immediate attention. I know you can understand why this is so. Home is where your day dawns and waking hours end. It shelters your physical body, ideas, secrets, possessions, and those you care for the most. You can't afford to expose your intimate spaces to attack through neglect. Think about your own home as you consider a few potential threats to your contentment there. Below are some identifiers of a detrimental location:

1. Uncleanness/clutter
2. Steady confrontation/violence/abuse
3. Unchecked depression/sadness/substance abuse
4. Absence of love, kindness or compassion (even if you live alone)
5. Excessive darkness
6. Neglect (no decorations, photos, or anything that makes it a home, not just a house)
7. Hazardous conditions (fear of being harmed at home or in the neighborhood)
8. Constant loud and disruptive noise
9. Financial insecurity (can't afford where you live)

10. Trauma or painful memories

You may not relate to anything on this list, but the point is that there are any number of specific factors that have direct bearing on life quality. Material things do not equate to happiness in and of themselves, although they can serve as enhancements. Owning an original of a fine piece of art means nothing if you are miserable as you walk by the wall on which it hangs. Home is the place where the heart exists. You should feel cradled and safe within its walls.

Order in the House!

Keeping your home clean promotes much needed order and security. Everyone has felt ill at ease when clutter has taken over an area of the home because of an ongoing project or other reason. (Read: You should see this desk right now!) You just can't get right until things are put back in place. You've heard the adage that what's going on outside reflects what's going on inside. When messiness becomes the norm that is very likely true.

There are times when housekeeping has to take a back seat to more pressing matters. When that happens, avoid leaving disarray for so long that it gets out of control or you get used to it. If it does, you could find yourself overwhelmed, which makes matters worse. Take one room or task at a time until your house and/or vehicle are in good shape. Find some help if you need to; your peace of mind is at stake.

Contention and Anger

Constant discord can leave you stressed and exhausted. Have you ever tried to enjoy a meal after an argument? It's next to impossible to even taste the food when your mind is in turmoil or your heart is aching. It's hard to focus and to create in a home where controversy has taken up permanent residence. Day after day of quarreling or having to defend yourself leads to a depressed psyche and generally cryptic outlook on life that follows you even when you are outside of your home.

Are peaceful days outweighed by those filled with turmoil? Only you can realistically judge if an imbalance exists. If you believe that conflict outweighs harmony, don't give in to defeat. Neither should you accept it as your ultimate destiny. Change the course!

Taking control of your environment is an intricate and sometimes lengthy process. It begs answers to questions such as who, what, where, why, and when. What factors caused the situation? You will need to address the causes of strife and dissonance. If you conclude that you have a part in what is going on, you have to explore your reasons for contributing to the dissention so that you can contribute to peace.

Another alternative is that the source of strife is someone else who lives under your roof. This is a situation in which you must be extremely cautious. It calls for tremendous strength and outside support to make decisions regarding people who share your home. Whether it is a roommate, friend, spouse, sibling, adult child, or other relative – use maximum care when you seek to determine how to handle the situation.

Choosing an option to rectify the issues which arise from another resident calls for wisdom. Depending on your relationship, you may find harmony can be recovered with hard work. If so, is that the outcome you both desire? What are each of you willing to do to maintain peace?

Will outside counselling help mediate some sort of resolution? Is separation inevitable? Should it be permanent? Could it be that a situation (such as financial or health matters), rather than the person, is the root of the turmoil in your home? Don't stop asking the difficult questions. And don't make a move until you get real answers.

There are so many variables with regard to these weighty matters. Never make a decision until you consider all things. Only you will know what will lead you to what is required in your household dynamic. Be truthful, fair, and open to avenues of enhancement. A word of caution: If you are in danger, don't wait. Secure your safety then work out the rest from a safe distance.

Ambiance

On a lighter note, making minor adjustments to your atmosphere may be all you need to increase positivity. There are many people who actually function at a higher level in surroundings that are in a state of chaos, or with loud background noise or darkness. But if that is not your experience, there are possible solutions.

Have you ever entered a room, either in your house or elsewhere, and had a strange feeling but couldn't pinpoint the cause? You may have passed through a space and suddenly felt sad or disoriented, seemingly without cause. If a certain part of your house causes your mood to drop, most likely it needs a little tweaking.

It doesn't have to take a lot of time and money to create elevating spaces, especially in the rooms in which you spend the most time. Remember, your surroundings correlate with your mind and emotions in subtle ways.

Colors, furniture placement, lighting, odors, dust, and sounds are just a few things that leave sensory impressions. Depending on the individual, exposure can elicit unhappy feelings, or even illness. The human mind stays mostly in a cluttered state; sometimes outside chaos exacerbates this condition and results in discomfort.

It is easier to insist upon and maintain calmness where you live than to endure a constant barrage of internal battles. Even when you are thinking of a thousand different problems, your body automatically becomes calmer when you enter a place of serenity. Your mind seeks out a source of peace from outside when it cannot grasp it from the inside. Again, this is why keeping order is beneficial.

Regularly check your home for ways to fashion variety, lightness, and soothing scents that solicit ease. You probably know that a lack of sunlight can be detrimental to

YOUR PURPOSE IN LIFE IS TO WIN!

your wellbeing. That also includes letting light into your home. Continual darkness can lead to clinical depression among other disorders. Go through your house and let in the sunlight sometimes, especially during the gloomy winter months. It will lift your spirits and also help eliminate dust mites.

Don't forget the bearing that smells have on your mood. Light candles or incense with fragrances that quiet you; oils and fragrance sticks also fill the air with pleasantries that clear your mind. Spend a day rearranging furniture in ways that are conducive to the healing, safe environment you need. Create relaxing little vignettes to read, take naps, or otherwise destress.

Invest in the most comfortable, eye pleasing furniture you can afford. Keep it clean and fresh smelling. Try switching out colors or patterns with covers and pillows in palates that draw you in and relax your mind. The idea is to produce a place where you can rest and thrive.

If you have children, it's not easy to keep your house neat and tidy. But it can stay reasonably clean and organized. Give children incentive to pick up behind themselves. Make their bedrooms and play spaces attractive (get their input) and they will be more willing to participate in its upkeep. Develop and enforce rules as to where they can play and for putting away their toys. Stay mindful of the example you set. They will be more likely to follow your lead when they see your commitment to keep an organized house.

Other Environments

There are other places you frequent outside of your living space. You have input regarding some of these areas, but most likely you don't. If, for example, you have the authority to adorn your work environment, apply the same principles as your home. Keep it clean, fresh, and tastefully decorated. Insist that co-workers respect your space.

What about places you go on your free time? Seeking out quality environments applies equally to these situations. You put your tranquility in jeopardy if you remain in places that make feel tense, unsafe, or antagonistic – wherever they may be. As much as I enjoy shopping, I am careful not to go (or stay) in overcrowded stores, as an example.

This also applies to your entertainment choices. If

you find yourself feeling upset, worried, or overall unhappy at an establishment, it is to your advantage to simply leave rather than risk bringing unhealthy energy back home to your haven. Do not lose sight of the fact that anything you come in contact with has an effect upon you, consciously or unconsciously. It is your duty to be sensitive to your senses.

Did you know you have the ability to carry the principles of a peaceful environment wherever you go? Your "mobile serenity" should follow you whenever you leave the house. Stand your ground for continued peace by avoiding conflicts with strangers in places like stores and while driving (that's a hard one for everybody I know).

If you are like me, and shy away from having long personal conversations with people you don't know, a hello and genuine smile only take a second and sets a serene tone. The gesture sends the message you are friendly but not chatty.

You will run into people in this world who simply want or need to be contentious. Don't try to talk them out of it. Just bask in your own inner peace and keep it moving

ENVIRONMENT

No adjustment to your home should be taken lightly. Do not take actions based solely on the opinions of other people or what you read or hear. Any suggestions or advice you take should be carefully evaluated see whether they are pertinent to your circumstances.

You cannot afford to make matters worse. You may conclude that you are satisfied with your situation and require few or no changes. In that case, all that is left to do is nurture and maintain your symphonic environment.

Whatever your conclusions and decisions, make creating ways to improve and maintain space lifestyle preference.

- Do you fear for your safety at home on some level? Don't ignore those feelings. Determine whether the feeling is coming from a specific person, or perhaps you fear the neighborhood in which you live. Get someone with whom you feel safe to assist you in making plans to promote your sense of safety. These plans can range from moving to installing added security to your home. Again, choose wisely based on your life circumstances.

- Consider modulating the sounds in your home. A constant barrage of loud voices or music might be affecting you in some manner.

- Are you in an environment which threatens your financial security? It is difficult to find peace in a home you cannot afford. You owe it to yourself to live without being scared. Consider downsizing your space if necessary and start fresh creating your ideal place in which you don't feel threatened.

- Do you spend time somewhere you cannot escape traumatic, painful memories? This can be a hindrance to healing and may even cause more damage. Watch for things like insomnia, crying, fear, nightmares, and other signs that you are suffering emotionally. Trust yourself to know when it may be time to consider leaving a space that elicits painful memories cause you steady discomfort and sadness.

7 TIME OUT

"Relaxing is hard work." ~Sheila Kay

Before you open your eyes each morning, your mind tells you that the day ahead is booked to capacity. You've become accustomed to juggling several things at once and you do so quite efficiently. But don't mistake the ease with which you perform with relaxation, which is vital to your mental and physical health. The pride you feel upon completion of day to day chores is not a substitute for down time. They don't count toward the things you do for sheer enjoyment that that are needed to provide balance.

Life is a series of electrifying highs and demoralizing lows. This rollercoaster ride can result in stress from trying to keep up with the twists and turns life delivers. To cope with the imbalances, make time to refresh the mind, body and soul. As the days appear to shrink even though the workload increases, you are in a clash to overcome the effects of everything from recessionary trends, voracious competition, attention to family, work and school obligations, and so much more.

97

In general, one way that relaxation can be distinguished from work is its restorative benefit. Whatever the activity, even if it involves exerting physical energy, you are renewed and feel calmer and looser afterward. The stakes are not as high as they are with work or family issues, allowing you to spend that time with less pressure. It feels as though you've been on a vacation, even if all you did was take an hour to go for a walk or something equally simple.

The importance of the need to unwind is also demonstrated by children, who must release energy during the course of the day. Parents frequently protest schools that have policies in place that allow teachers to withhold recess as punishment. Why?

Because the benefits of free time far outweigh any infraction by most students. Extensive research has concluded that recess is vital for the physical, emotional, social, and intellectual development of students. How much more so does the overworked adult need some form of daily retreat?

To refresh ensures that you can continue taking care of yourself, family, business, and spiritual matters so much more effectively than if you are overburdened. Keeping anxiety levels in check includes recognizing you need some relaxation and then arranging to make it happen, even if you only have small periods of time to do so.

It is true that small levels of stress serve as motivation to perform well. I know people, including myself, that work best when they are under pressure. But staying at a high level of alert all day, every day, can result in burnout.

In adults, this can take many forms such as breakdowns, depressed or angry mood, and inability to perform. Make relaxation a priority because:

- You will sleep better when you make it a habit to relax before bed.
- Mood swings are less frequent with people who enjoy leisure time.
- Long term physical health can be improved with less stress and more free time.
- People who take breaks have sharper concentration and better memory.

- Consciously relaxing will help you cope better and bounce back in the event of misfortune.

- You will become familiar with and enjoy the part of you that is fun and carefree.

The majority of hard working people in the world do not have the time or resources (or desire) to unplug from life for long periods of time. However, you cannot afford to neglect handling pressure and engaging in leisure activities. So you have to develop a personal approach for taking control at a level that is suited to your own needs. Be creative and plan activities that bring your anxiety down a few pegs with quick fixes you can do even in the middle of the day, such as breathing techniques.

Controlling Your Breathing

Do you know how to create a measure of stillness any time of the day or night? Learning to control your breathing is an excellent way to calm down and destress. How does breathing relate to the way you feel? When you are fretful or under pressure, your breathing is shallow and fast. This reduces the amount of oxygen that gets to your organs. Your body responds immediately to this deprivation which, if unrestrained, can in time lead to serious physical and emotional anxiety symptoms.

Have you ever had unexplained headaches, upset stomach, or tension in your neck? It is possible that you are stressed or anxious and not breathing properly. Take note if you have episodes in which you stop breathing or breathe sporadically and shallow. Don't ignore dizziness or chest pains when they occur. Remain conscious of your breathing and work to maintain control. Make each breath count towards keeping you as healthy as possible to avoid these and other symptoms.

On average, humans take between 17,000-30,000 breaths each day. Most healthy people do not pay attention to this natural bodily function. But even a person in perfect health can undergo changes in breathing under certain extreme conditions, like a sudden emergency or disturbance. Emotions like anger, surprise, or fear can also throw off the natural rhythm which is ideal for the individual.

One technique that has helped people is to put one hand on your upper chest and the other on your stomach. Breathe in deeply enough to make your stomach rise; it should fall back when you breathe out. Create a steady breathing rhythm by taking in the same amount of air with each breath you take in. Make a conscious effort to slow your breathing. Although it may take a few tries for this to feel comfortable, with practice you may be able to control your breathing.

Slowing your breathing ensures you are getting oxygen to vital organs throughout your body, such as the lungs and brain. When these and other organs have sufficient oxygen, you immediately feel a sense of calm and wellbeing. You are able to function at a higher level even while under the pressure that your day may bring.

Get Away Right Where You Are

Since the majority of your day is spent working or taking care of family or business, it is not always possible to physically take time off when you need it. Again, use your creativity to think of small, discreet "vacations" to blow off steam and have a little fun on the spot.

Below are a few suggestions to get you started.

1. Attend a private "concert". Pick your

favorite performer and play a few of their songs. If you are not able to play them on your device, then concentrate and sing along in your mind, focusing on every note.

2. Go to the comedy club. Similar to the "concert". Think of some of the funniest jokes or stories you know. If possible, share a good laugh with a friend or coworker.

3. If you haven't done so, place visual objects of your favorite people and places in your work space. When you feel overwhelmed, take a break to look at the memorabilia and recall special moments.

4. Indulge in a little treat (keep something tasty just for you in your desk or locker) and slowly savor every bite.

5. Close your eyes, take a few deep cleansing breaths and stretch your muscles to relieve tension throughout the work day.

Basically, it's all about freeing your mind, even for a moment or two. You may be fortunate enough to be able to go for brief walks, work out, or even grab a short catnap at your desk to get relief from difficult or mundane chores. A little can go a long way. Find something to tide you over until you can get home and get in an even more relaxed state.

Barriers to Loosening Up

Ideally, you have no trouble at all finding fun, restorative activities to fill up your free hours. Research has shown, however, that the majority of hard working adults find it difficult to discipline themselves to let go on a regular basis. There are several reasons this is becoming so widespread and problematic.

Lack of finances prevents some people from developing a routine pattern of taking a break. But for anyone determined to do so, recreation and relaxation can be inexpensive or even free. Naturally, there are things you can do at home such as hobbies, watching television, entertaining company, playing games, listening to music and more. But maybe you want to get out of the house.

Walking in a park or elsewhere is free and also good for you. Most city parks also have tennis courts, basketball courts, baseball diamonds and other sports if you are so inclined, at little or no cost to residents. If you are not the athletic type, then take a picnic, book, laptop/tablet (for reading or movies-not work), and chill out in the fresh air for a while.

Every season of the year, most municipalities sponsor recreational activities such as music concerts, holiday festivals, fireworks, and fairs of all kinds. Go online or watch the local news for the latest happenings in your area. Consider joining groups with interests similar to yours. You can have fun and also meet accountability partners who will make sure you have a good time every now and then.

You may be surprised to know that by far, most obstacles to relaxation are not money, time, or even poor health. It is possible to block your own way to those restful moments of freedom that everyone needs. Take a look at the questions below. Any answers you give in the affirmative may indicate you are the culprit.

Do you have difficulty saying "no" to requests from others?

You could be putting too much on your plate. Choose your "yeses" carefully.

Is playing online games a regular part of your workday?

Mixing play in between working delays completing your work. Finish work so you can have actual free time.

Are you the person who everyone comes to with their gossip or drama?

You have enough of your own issues; don't let just anyone suck up your precious free time over nonsense. Set boundaries and stay within them.

How much planning do you put into scheduling relaxation?

If you don't plan ahead, you are not committed to making it happen – and it won't.

Have you convinced yourself that you have no time, money, or need to take time off?

You will either take time off voluntarily or your mind and body will force you to do so eventually. Take the high road. Love yourself by making fun a priority.

The benefits go beyond having a brief respite. You deserve a well-rounded life that includes participation in actions for simple joy, not because you are on the clock or under threat of discipline.

Sometimes it is hard to see the things you've done while you are in the midst of doing them. Make sure you reflect on all you have accomplished while you are in a relaxed state. It will make you feel proud and give you all the more incentive keep going.

You must be conscientious in preparing for this aspect of your life to come to fruition. Make it a priority. Do what it takes to make it happen. Delegate work when you can, reschedule if possible, and let go of nonessential duties to find some time to do what you want to do. Dare yourself to do something enjoyable and different.

Do not pressure yourself in any way when it comes to recreational time, because it will defeat the purpose. Avoid planning activities that cost more than you can afford (in time or money). It will only cause stress later. Walk your own repose path. What is exciting and entertaining for you is your personal choice to make. Whatever it may be, enjoy yourself and return invigorated and inspired!

TIME OUT

In this chapter you were reminded to tap into your carefree side. You have demonstrated that you are an efficient, competent and responsible worker. Now you've decided to master the art of rest and recovery. Adapt these exercises to fit your lifestyle.

- For 24 hours, keep track of the amount of time you spend checking emails, texts, social media, news, and other information on your electronic devices. Total the time. Try to cut the time by at least a third and devote that time (no matter how little) to relaxation, meditation, recreation or simply doing nothing.

- Where would you go on your dream vacation (or your next dream vacation if you've already been)? Spend some free time researching everything about the destination as though you will be traveling in the near future. It's a fun way to expand your knowledge and to give yourself something to look forward to.

- Partner with someone you trust and create a calendar of leisure activities the two of you can do together. Take turns choosing what you will do so you can discover new things or places the other person does that you might enjoy.

8 HEALTH

"When you don't feel good, you can't do good."

~Sheila Kay

If you possess the gift of perfect health, you have nothing of greater value. You are able to do whatever you desire without restriction. If this is you, surely you are taking full advantage of your vigor and living life to the maximum. Congratulations! May you enjoy continued wholeness.

In reality, absolute perfect health is a rare commodity. As such, this chapter addresses strategies for living your best despite (or because of) whatever challenges you face. Naturally, prevention is the best medicine for all manner of ailments. But heredity, environment, age, lifestyle and other factors do effect the health of millions each year.

Causes include chronic physical or mental health conditions, disease, injury, or the effects of getting older. Below are four main areas which effect your body, whether or not you have an illness:

1. Eating

2. Rest/Sleep

3. Exercise

4. Stress/Emotions

Food

The United States Department of Agriculture estimated that $71 billion is spent on medical costs related to improper nutrition alone. Relatively few people can honestly say they don't have some type of issue with food. Either you love it, hate it, eat the wrong kinds of food, or don't consume enough of the food that is good for you.

A lot of people possess the sheer willpower that drives them to eat a consistent, well balanced diet. These people are usually terrific motivators who are willing to share tips on their successful dietary habits. So if you struggle with your eating behaviors, connect with someone who is willing to mentor you, or consider a nutritional professional for assistance.

It is common for individuals to struggle when it comes to eating. The stakes are even higher if you have disease or illness. Poor dietary habits will catch up with the healthiest person eventually, but for others it can make health worse or lead to avoidable death. A health condition does not halt your resolve or ability to win. But by no means can or should you ignore a health problem either. What you can do is incorporate sensible and practical tactics to enable you to continue your forward momentum.

Below are some tips you can try, but *not before you have consulted with your doctor.* The advice of your physician may vary due to your particular illness and its severity.

1. The doctor's orders are your first orders. Listen carefully and follow the advice you are given. Ask questions and keep asking if you need clarification on any matter.

2. You may be referred to a nutritionist to help manage your diet. Again, don't hesitate to ask pointed questions. If you have allergies to, or strongly dislike, a certain food that is recommended, let them know so that they can provide the correct alternatives.

3. Try to keep the food you should eat handy. Buy non-perishables in bulk or at least purchase two of the items

so you do not run out and have to eat something you shouldn't.

4. Messing up doesn't mean giving up. If you fall off of your suggested diet, start again.

5. Prepare approved "to go" packages to take with you in case you are delayed while you are away from home. They will prevent you from getting too hungry and eating the wrong food.

6. It is easy to skip meals when you are busy. Stop what you are doing, no matter how important, and give your body the nutrients it requires for you to feel your best. You need that nourishment to have the strength to perform.

Rest/Sleep

To awake after a refreshing night of sound sleep is a precious commodity. Yet, as the years pass, it becomes more elusive (or does it escape just me?). You cannot function at optimal levels if your body is not getting regular restorative sleep. That is not to say you *don't* function. Millions of people put in twelve or more hour days on very little sleep.

In reality, this lifestyle eventually causes a litany of health problems and is reported to shorten life expectancy. Sleep deprivation is also well known as a form of torture. Even if you don't miss out on sleep intentionally, your body does not know or care. It joins your mind in becoming distressed and unhealthy from lack of rest.

You may have one of several sleep disorders if you are actually trying to sleep but cannot. There are about ten types of insomnia, three of which are most common. Sleep onset insomnia is when you have difficulty falling asleep. Sleep maintaining insomnia prevents you from staying asleep. Early morning awakening is evidenced by consistently waking up after only a little sleep.

Don't be tempted to diagnose why you are missing out on solid rest. Give your doctor a detailed report on your sleep patterns in order to get the proper treatment or advice that is best for *you*. Your health, age, lifestyle, and other factors will be monitored and evaluated.

A sleep specialist or other medical professional can find a potential underlying physical or psychological cause of your insomnia that you don't know about. Medical assessment is a crucial step; what is enough (or too much) sleep for one person can be totally different in your case.

Life goes on whether you sleep or not. You have various responsibilities as well as your purpose to pursue. There is an exhausting list of possible reasons you can't rest or sleep. Illness, worry, strategizing, and a crying baby are a mere few. Nonetheless, at times you have to keep it moving without regard to your rest broken state.

But sleep is not a luxury, it is a necessity. Without it, your body will force you to shut down. While you work on getting to the root of your restlessness, you can look into some techniques to try until you find the solution.

Do some research on relaxation methods that you think could be of benefit. It is said that different types of meditation can relieve stress, which could be a reason for your sleeplessness. If physical pain keeps you up at night, find solutions to ease your suffering. Ask your doctor what medication is safe for you to take to relieve the hurt.

If you choose not to take medication, perhaps you can get relief from natural methods like changing sleep positions, applying heat or cold (per doctor's instructions), herbal supplements, or a change in diet (again, ask your doctor).

Try to steal some quiet time during the day, especially on the days you haven't slept well the night before. Are you as comfortable as possible when you retire to bed at night? Adjust environmental factors like lighting, noise, temperature, and orderliness as needed.

If you can't sleep without background noise, be sure your television, audio, or other source is on low volume. Make sure the channel you choose does not broadcast violence or other disruptive transmissions throughout the wee hours that can seep into your psyche and disturb your slumber.

Exercise

No one can escape the need for their body to get exercise on a regular basis. There's not an organ or system or system within you that does not require exertion to stay viable.

The type, frequency, and amount of time you exercise are determined by several personalized factors. They include your age, weight and health status. What you desire to do, or what your friends do, are not necessarily determinative of your requirements. Once again, this is an area in which you must "seek advice from your health care professional", as they say.

Once you have clearance, find something you like (or don't hate) to do. Walking is one of the least expensive, easiest, and most effective ways to put in time to take care of your body. Swimming and water aerobics are good choices too and have little impact on your joints.

Contemplate participating in other activities like team sports (even ping pong or a similar table game) with other people who will keep you motivated. If you would rather work out in the privacy of your home, put on a fitness program or some music and keep up to the extent you are able. Put together your own gym for as little or as much as you can afford.

Don't neglect to keep your mind in shape. Challenge yourself to explore new subjects and push further in areas you are familiar. Brain games are fun and helpful in sharpening the mind. So are inquisitive children; don't brush off all of their questions by telling them to look up the answers. If you happen to not know an answer, research the subject with your child or grandchild.

The bottom line is you must exercise. This is not something you don't know; it is written to simply nudge you in the direction you are already aware you need to go. The good news for those who don't live for the burn is that any extra movement you make and steps you are able to take throughout the day have at least some merit.

You don't have to do an hour of extreme cardio at full speed every six hours to improve your health - unless you enjoy doing that. Just move. If working out is one of your favorite things in this world to do, you are obviously very good at it. Please find a friend who can use your help and encouragement in setting up a fitness plan they can follow.

Stress/Emotions

If you are living and breathing on this earth, stress comes with the territory. The level of disquiet you experience depends upon the situation you face. More importantly, your reaction (or lack of it) is dictated by your emotional makeup.

So although you can't avoid it, you've got to do your part in not letting stress get the best of you. Start now to avoid burning out your vital organs and your peace of mind due to constant emotional overload. Map out a line of attack ahead of time for the times when sudden stressful conditions arise. Practice the control it will take to swallow your pride, even if you are right, and to walk away from heated debates or arguments.

Exit the freeway or turn the corner when you encounter a rage filled motorist looking for a fight or almost causing an accident. Those are not the type of battles you are here to win. So too, leave unkind or untruthful media posts or in-person senseless rumors without reply. Ignore ignorance and pettiness from any source. You'll know when you have to take a stand. When you do, take a deep breath, state your point, and leave it alone.

Very often, contentious, high stress circumstances are not your fault and are unavoidable. This happens a lot with friends and family misunderstandings or emergency situations. In these instances, slow down and carefully deliberate the course you will take to prevent becoming overtaken while you are in the midst of whatever is happening.

Mentally negotiate alternatives that could lessen

the strain. Can you resolve or delegate some elements of the problem to break it up into smaller portions? Can you take action to resolving some of the tension, like making peace with someone close to you?

Who hasn't gone through financial, health, family, work problems that take time before they are resolved? It is impossible to turn off a switch and destress when you are faced with weighty matters. What will get you through is support, careful strategy, and patience.

Investigate new methods for alleviating pressure that others have tried and met with success. Try not to keep emotions bottled up inside, or take on everything by yourself. Reach out to a friend or family member willing to let you vent your feelings. Don't hesitate for an instant to get medical help and treatment if you find yourself constantly nervous or panicked.

Humor is an excellent way to minimize a taxing moment. Sometimes you can use your sense of humor to your advantage to defuse a situation. Set aside your pride and take one for the team by laughing at yourself. Helping other people is equally rewarding and relaxing. A good cleansing cry can ease tension and frustration in some cases.

If you have an ongoing health concern, or have cared for someone who does, you can be a blessing to someone who is facing the same situation. Your reassurance and experience may be just the medicine another person needs to face another day with courage. You are unique but not alone, so don't isolate yourself because of an illness. Don't shy away from those who are not well if you are fortunate enough to be in robust health.

Exercise relieves stress, as does eating right and getting proper rest. As you can see, all of the subjects covered in this chapter tie in to one another with regard to your health.

Your health takes precedence over any goals you have set. Don't even think about risking your current state of health to meet a deadline, pursue a dream, or to gain prosperity. If you don't take care of yourself, nothing else really matters. What is a win without the victor being able to celebrate it?

HEALTH

By this point in the book you are getting a picture of how various parts of your life form a composite of your existence. You recognize that success is an evolutionary process. You'll change, rearrange, and redefine the elements to make yourself even more amazing as time passes.

Then, your courage increases as you skillfully revamp again and again for renewed success. Stay as healthy as possible to keep up your strength and stamina.

- If you haven't done so in the past year or two, start making health appointments. Include physical, dental, vision, and any other necessary checkups.
- Be honest if you are having an unknown symptom that you are ignoring. Get it looked at by a medical professional.

- Consider creating a wellness calendar. Choose something to do each day for the betterment and maintenance of your mental or physical health. Tasks can include visiting loved ones, donating time or items to somebody less fortunate, trying a new exercise, reading something new, etc.

- Decide now that neglecting yourself is no longer an option. Embrace it as a lifetime commitment.

9 PERSONAL SURVEY

"You must challenge yourself if no one else is around to do it for you. It is necessary to keep you sharp and to escape complacency and procrastination." ~Sheila Kay

This book is not intended to cover every possible scenario you encounter. Rather, it is a compilation of various situations to which people in general can relate on some level. The idea is to offer encouragement to any and everyone who has chosen to fight for their right to a brighter life. Hopefully, it also served as a reminder that you are not isolated in what you experience.

Although humans share many commonalities, their individual day to day life practices are as different as their fingerprints. Your life is made up of personal intricacies and how you react to them in your own special way. That is why it is important to get an exclusive snapshot to serve as a guide to formulating your plan. The choice you make in a given situation will be entirely different from the one someone else makes when faced with the same issue.

Below are several statements, each containing a blank line. You can write them down on a separate paper or save in a document. Take your time and fill in each blank with your honest truth. Remember, your reality is not held in judgment. No one has to see what you have written. This exercise will give you guidance how to identify, organize, and then prioritize just a very few of the numerous issues you deal with in your life. It is a starting point in the completion of your customized representation.

Survey Says!

My greatest obstacle at this moment is _____.

I can _____ as a step toward overcoming my obstacle or functioning despite its existence.

_____ are my greatest supporters/allies and will be willing to help me thrive.

I know my ultimate strength is _____.

I will make plans to assist _____ in reaching their

goals or I will provide then with something they need.

My greatest weakness is _____.

What scares me the most is _____.

_____ will be beneficial in helping me strengthen areas of weakness.

Today, I will _____ to reward myself.

When I speak negatively about myself, I will replace the word(s)_____ with _____.

I choose to work on breaking the habit of _____, which is impeding my progress.

Starting today, _____ will be on my list of things to do each day.

When I feel hopeless, I will _____ to change my perspective.

If I am totally honest, _____ is doing me harm in one way or another.

This week I will commit to _____ to relieve some of the stress I feel.

I realize _____ might need to be looked at by a doctor, so I will no longer ignore it.

When you are finished, read the completed statements aloud. Hearing the words may spark life into your desire to do what you've written. Refer to these statements over time to track what changes you have made. As always, add or subtract your own ideas so that this too fits your life like a glove.

Do you write down your thoughts, ideas, and feelings as often as you like? If not, this is a good way to actually see from the outside what goes on inside of your mind. Some people shy away from journaling, mistakenly believing they have to be a writer to try this form of expression. However, to journal is simply to put down the thoughts which have already existed in your mind. There is no need to be concerned with proper grammar, structure, or even spelling.

If you really do not like to write, make recordings or even videos when you feel the need to vent or express ideas. Oftentimes, letting something out is cathartic; you may be able to focus better once you've cleared your mind. Be creative in making your mark in the world. You never know who may benefit from what you share.

If you have the impression that all of this is a never-ending process, you are entirely correct. A life in motion sees ups, downs, and everything in between. But it is never stagnant. Even at rest you are working to renew yourself for the next great phase. Though it may not seem so, that is actually terrific news. Because the alternative is a life with nothing to look forward to except another day of regret.

10 THE COOL DOWN

As it stands, you have reached the end of a book that has provided you with insights and inspiration. By doing so you've added to your existing life plan, which is to be the best imaginable. Well done!

It takes courage to tackle the issues covered here, such as accepting who you are without reservation, and navigating relationships. You are even more determined to make taking care of yourself the first priority. Always appreciate that, no matter what, you have a fantastic lifetime friend that lives right inside of you.

The exercises at the end of the chapters were designed to challenge you to take a deep breath and dive deeply into the waters which are composed of the lifeblood of your existence. You should proudly feel the burn as you are putting in the effort to make yourself mentally meaner, leaner, and stronger.

No longer do you fear the known or unknown. You possess a keen awareness that real life comes with joys and sorrows. But you have decided to keep your eye on the brightest star you can imagine. It awaits you, even in the darkness.

Hopefully, finishing this book will result in some form of positive change. Maybe you've decided to face a mental or emotional challenge head on. It's possible you have chosen to make health changes for the better. Celebrate the fact you've selected to change, which is by no means easy. It's even more likely that the book served to reinforce what you have begun already.

Whether you have committed to some new changes, or confirmed changes that are already in progress, you're a fierce combatant for life. After any fight or workout, there are certain steps that must be taken to avoid injury. Since this is the last chapter of the book, I think it is a good time for you take the first one - the cool down.

As you know, when you finish physical exercise, the worst thing you can do is to suddenly come to a standstill. Although you may have completed the physical activity, the workout is not really over. You must lower your heart rate slowly, at a steady pace, by walking around or doing some other low key activity. If you don't, you put yourself at risk of feeling sick, enduring muscle soreness, or inflicting injury.

Now is the optimal time for you to progressively

process what you have read. If certain subjects in the book struck a chord more than others, go back and read the chapter again. Add your own ideas to incorporate the information into what you are doing currently. Or simply meditate on what you envision to be the marvelous future which lays before you.

Don't put pressure on yourself by attempting to tackle too much. Listen to yourself with newfound trust. Give yourself time to develop what you've read. Relax in the knowledge that you have time to review and renew your life to attain whatever you want to happen.

Even before you read this book, you did the majority of the work to lay the foundation for conquest. You have time to cool down before you spring into action.

Take Another Good Stretch

You have years of practice at stretching yourself in order to accomplish your goals. You have surprised yourself many times when you've kept going, even when you thought you could go no further. Staying active kept your mind from becoming stagnant and rigid. Now that you have finished this particular workout, it is time to stretch again.

Stretching your physical body prevents the muscles from shrinking. Your muscles can grow bigger, your circulation is improved, and you get stronger. So it is with life. Continue to reach a little farther toward your ambitions each day.

Take small, easy steps in the realms of your reality. Challenge your mind, body, and spirit in an area which you believe you've reached the pinnacle. There's more for you to conquer than you know. Extend yourself, because what's beyond what you can see is yours for the taking.

Replenish

The cool down phase includes creating ways to renew and refresh your mind and body. Whether you know it or not, you have expended an enormous amount of energy. As you prosper, you will need even more energy for the next season. Here are a few ways to get a quick recharge:

- You need time alone. This may take some arranging, but make it a point to indulge yourself with some unashamedly, reenergizing "me time".

Even an hour to yourself makes a big difference.

- Enlighten someone you care about by sharing something which will trigger them to renew their efforts to live optimally. The added benefit is that your energy level rises too when you speak on a subject of which you are passionate.

- All winners get a reward for victory. Gift yourself some sort of a prize for the undefeated life you are creating.

Some professional boxers claim to experience the worse physical pain or discomfort the day after a fight. Even though their bodies get plummeted during the bout, adrenalin seems to delay the reaction to the physical pain. They continue round after round, bloody and battered, until the fight is over.

Keep that in mind as you go forward in the battle to win. Inevitably, you will take some hits that hurt. Accept that life will always bring rough challenges from which you must (and will) recover. Being the fighter you are, you will acquire bruises, but they are not a death sentence. As you heal, keep your eyes focused ahead where more contests await. You have in no way lost that fight or the ones to come.

Stop the Presses!

Every day something different threatens to destroy what I am trying to build. Do you have the same experience? Can you recognize an attempt to be pulled into a state of apprehension as you reach for excellence? That's what happens with contenders. There is always a target on our backs to attempt to snatch what is rightfully ours.

One thing (among many) I say quite often is, "I'm not pressed." I use that to express that I am not desperate or worried about an issue, person, or whatever I am referring to at the time. The words are part of my personal verbal confirmation that by no means do I have to compromise who I am in exchange for gain or affirmation.

That sentiment doesn't translate into me being better than anyone else. Rather, it indicates now I'm spending whatever energy and resources I have on living my best. My best involves attention and devotion to the ones I love and care for, (including myself). Being my finest self also keeps me very busy striving to be true to my many life's purposes. Beyond that, I don't have much left. What works for me, is for me.

Over the years I have toyed with other words that contain the word 'pressed'. Just for the fun of it, over time I have added them to my stance of not being frantic or tossed back and forth based on what other people think from one day to the next. Below are some playful affirmations for you to recall to help keep stress, doubt, and people pleasing in check.

Speak the following truths along with your current affirmations.

I DECLARE THAT I AM NOT:

1. **Pressed**. There is nothing that someone else has or can do to me that will cause me to compromise who I am as a person. I am not pressed into a state of panic in any aspect of my life. Therefore, I will work at maintaining a relaxed state, knowing that what I am intended to have will come my way in time.

2. **Oppressed.** No circumstance or person is allowed to torment or torture me. I will endure adversity that comes my way, even though I know there will be times it feels unbearable. I will always challenge oppressive thoughts or speaking as I wait for the situation to improve. I am not burdened with foolish pride. I gratefully accept help when needed.

3. **Impressed.** At a minimum, I admire myself equally as much as I do other people. I recognize and congratulate excellence in myself and others. I am uninhibited and generous in giving honest compliments. I have no problem receiving sound advice without feeling threatened or insecure. I am captivated with my inner winner and accept that I leave a positive impression on everyone I encounter.

4. **Suppressed.** The days of feeling inhibited by fear or intimidation are over. I will openly and fully express

who I am in a spirit of graciousness and humility mixed with confidence. I will not shrink away from success and vow to be generous with all I have been given.

5. **Compressed.** I am bigger than life with no insoluble limits. Whatever state I find myself, all I have to do is search for the specific means which will relieve any debilitating pressure as I await solutions. I aim high and wide as I walk uninhibited in my irreplaceable purpose. I am relieved of the obligation to receive or be affected by either subtle or overt senseless negativity thrown in my direction.

You probably have a great list of declarations and affirmation to which you refer each day. I also soak up inspirational and positive messages. They serve to counter-maneuver the enemies of calmness that are so abundant in this world. I am thankful for the variety of people on this planet who also make it their life's work to plant motivation in some form or another. I'm convinced that you are among them.

Recap

Here are some takeaways from the book with a few additional points on the same topics which were not included in the chapters.

Chapter 1-Self Acceptance

You have the choice of being your best friend or your worst enemy. Acceptance starts with being brutally honest about yourself without judgement or comparison. This is followed by giving yourself the same sort of kindness and nurturing you give to the people you love the most.

Not only must you love yourself, but you also have to LIKE who you are! The opinions of others either simply confirm or deny what you already know. So they should not take up days or years of deliberation to contemplate their validity or necessity. It doesn't take a lot of boasting and convincing for your greatness to be evident. Real quality speaks volumes in and of itself. Demonstrate pride and dignity in your true self daily with no reservations.

Chapter 2-You Are What You Do

Defining what you want to do or learn outside of your regular responsibilities takes true dedication. Habits, especially those that add nothing to your goals, can be changed. As you discover what you want to do, devote your energy into what you need to make it happen.

Don't dismiss anything you do as minimal or insignificant. Everything has reason or validation. What you may view as the least of your accomplishments may be, in fact, the most significant when it comes to forging a new path.

Chapter 3-Relationship Proximity

No one escapes interaction with other humans, it is just a matter of the degree of closeness. Evaluate the importance and proximity to you of the people in your life regularly.

While it is true you can choose friends but not family, you can decide if putting distance between you and another person is the only way to keep peace. The relationships which are mutually beneficial, with a blood relative or not, should be sheltered and nourished. Don't take them for granted.

Chapter 4-Mind Control

The mind is on the front line of the war to attain contentment. Therefore, expect to suffer the first and hardest attacks upon your mindset. Don't take what you think lightly; your thoughts are prerequisite to your actions.

You can't totally control what goes on in your head but you can put up a strong defense against dangerous imaginations. Guard your mind whenever possible; don't make it easy for pessimism to stay. When it does, be ready to charge!

Chapter 5-Time Out

Relaxation should be counted among the essentials in life. Fortunately, it affords the most flexibility with regard to the type of activity, amount of money spent, and length of time taken.

Living a life without enjoyment outside of regular responsibilities downgrades its eminence. It can be compared to eating meals only in pill form. The nutrients are there but you don't get to relish the great taste. Refreshing yourself is not a step you can skip so make it happen.

Chapter 6-Environment

Your gratification is intertwined with your surroundings, from the air you breathe, where and how you live, to the people around you. Environment requires special attention; its effects can sneak up on you without you realizing that a correlation exists.

Develop a sense of the impact that a location has upon how you feel. This does not only apply to any an adverse reaction you may have, but also be aware whether certain people or places motivate and rejuvenate you enough to frequent them often for added support.

Chapter 7-Health

Neglecting your health, for any reason, is just as harsh as abuse. Not only that, but not taking care of yourself is a sure way to miss the mark when it comes to living whole. You deserve as much wellness as possible. People who care for you also want and need you to stay healthy.

Physical and mental exercise, managing stress, and nutrition are crucial to your health. And without proper rest, it is impossible to function effectively and consistently. "Sleep is that golden chain that ties our bodies together."-Thomas Dekker

Final Thoughts

Like anyone else, you will second guess your ability to push past your limits. You might ask yourself, "How can I concentrate on achieving monumental success in this world if I struggle to simply exist?"

The question is valid and relevant. After all, there are so many other things that command your attention. How can you manage what needs to be done immediately while planning something that won't happen until the future?

For every day that dawns, the former 24 hours is considered the past. As for the daily struggles of life, taking on one problem at a time is definitely a wise approach.

Look, or patiently wait, for resolutions to problems, rather than attempt to tackle everything at once. Untie the complicated knots in your life with tenacity and deliberation. Remember, each day you make it through is a testimony to your greatness. In that sense, your future is now.

You are further along than you were yesterday, which places you closer to your destiny. Meanwhile, you have the privilege to live life in motion, filled with discovery and creativity. Sure, you will question yourself along the way. But never doubt that you exist for purpose.

As time passes, you will become progressively adept at making targeted choices to keep your life in balance. It is up to you to set the rules for what governs your life. They are easily identifiable because they always add, and not subtract, from your concerns. You will competently set boundaries when needed as you take command of where your life is headed.

Continually make investments in your purpose, using anything you can get your hands on. Keep reading books, attend seminars or conferences, and accept help from people who are eager for you to win. Connect with like-minded people by joining relevant groups.

Evaluate your perspectives so that you are certain you are focusing on what is important. Stay alert; opportunities for fulfillment are everywhere. Don't be shy or ashamed to talk about your plans in case there is someone listening who can be a valuable ally.

Have you ever seen an entertainer drop the microphone and walk away after a performance? Or heard someone say they left everything on the stage? These gestures demonstrate that they have given their all. They indicate that they are confident they did their best no matter what others think.

Enjoy your chance at winning with each breath you take. Give life everything you've got, even if the deafening applause you hear is your own. However, unlike a singing or dancing contest, dedicating your all to everything you do and say is a no-lose scenario. It is the definition of a successful and purposeful life in a nutshell.

Close your eyes for just a moment and visualize the realization of your dreams. Did your heart quicken with the excitement of what is to come? You got a mere glimpse of your one-of-a-kind prime masterpiece coming together to engender a portrait of triumph.

YOUR PURPOSE IN LIFE IS TO WIN!

About the Author

Sheila Kay is an editor, ghostwriter, and business owner. Born and raised in Detroit, MI, she has lived in the Metro Atlanta, GA area for ten years. Among her interests are travel, cooking, reading, and a variety of charitable endeavors.

Her online retail store, The Undefeated Me™ Shop, features hundreds of products and merchandise which celebrate the championship spirit. As a blossoming movement, The Undefeated Me™ represents conquering adversity and promoting excellence and strength in every aspect of life.

Ms. Kay is the co-founder of an upcoming nonprofit organization to provide resources, support, and job skills training to homeless Atlanta residents seeking to return to the workforce.

Her memoir, PTSD and the Undefeated Me, was released in 2015. The story chronicled her life prior to and since her diagnosis of Post Traumatic Stress Disorder related to a personal tragedy.

Since then she has become increasingly involved in advocacy and awareness concerns related to mental illness among civilians, as well as lending support to veterans and their families.

The Undefeated Me™

The Undefeated Me™ Gifts and Merchandise

Author Sheila Kay's online shop was inspired by the overwhelming response to her book, *PTSD and the UNDEFEATED ME,* a memoir of her life. Readers of the book made it a point to write Ms. Kay about how they were inspired by her determination to fight for life. Some shared their own life experiences and were appreciative of the openness and hope Ms. Kay related in her book.

The store offers hundreds of unique products, in over 15 departments, that express and promote a movement that consists of overcoming hardship and maintaining a winning spirit.

Shop for housewares, clothing, stationary, automobile accessories, jewelry and so much more. Each item proudly displays the commitment to live without a mindset of defeat.

Take a look at the exclusive inspirational merchandise offered. Visit The Undefeated Me™ Facebook page: www.facebook.com/theundefeatedme or AristocratPublishing.com

www.ingramcontent.com/pod-product-compliance
Lightning Source LLC
Chambersburg PA
CBHW060015050426
42448CB00012B/2770